BEST RESUMES FOR
EDUCATIONAL
PROFESSIONALS

BEST RESUMES FOR EDUCATIONAL PROFESSIONALS

Kim Marino

John Wiley & Sons, Inc.

New York • Chichester • Brisbane • Toronto • Singapore

This publication is designed to provide accurate and
authoritative information in regard to the subject
matter covered. It is sold with the understanding that
the publisher is not engaged in rendering legal, accounting,
or other professional services. If legal advice or other
expert assistance is required, the services of a competent
professional person should be sought.

Library of Congress Cataloging-in-Publication Data:

Marino, Kim, 1951–
    Best resumes for educational professionals / by Kim Marino.
        p.   cm.
    Published simultaneously in Canada.
    Includes index.
    ISBN 0-471-31144-8 (pbk. : alk. paper)
    1. Teachers—Employment. 2. Résumés (Employment) I. Title.
LB1780.M37   1994
    808'.06665—dc20   93-47212

Printed in the United States of America

10 9 8 7 6 5 4 3 2

Preface

As the founder of Just Resumes® Writing Service and author of five resume books, including *Best Resumes for Accountants and Financial Professionals* (John Wiley & Sons, January 1994), *Resumes for the Health Care Professional* (John Wiley & Sons, January 1993), and *Just Resumes® 200 Powerful and Proven Successful Resumes to Get That Job* (John Wiley & Sons, November 1991), I am readily acquainted with the resume needs of the educational professional. My own files contain resume samples from a wide range of teaching professionals, administrators, counselors, and media specialists. I have stayed in touch with this field and have brought my knowledge to bear in *Best Resumes for Educational Professionals*.

This book includes more than 100 resume samples for teachers, administrators, counselors, and media specialists of private and public elementary and secondary schools, and postsecondary community colleges. Both traditional and new positions are addressed with a step-by-step guide to the fine art of creating a professionally designed resume. I have also included valuable inside tips and facts, all of which are specific to the educational profession.

This book provides cover letter and thank-you letter samples and how-to information to complete the resume packet. Later chapters expand on job trends, job searching, and interviewing tips for educational professionals.

Whether you're a educational professional returning to the workforce, changing careers, or moving up, or you're a college student or recent graduate entering the educational profession, I am confident this book is one of the best investments you'll ever make.

KIM MARINO

Fort Collins, Colorado

Acknowledgments

I'd like to express my gratitude to the following educational professionals who have been instrumental in helping me with my research in the field of education: Eric Reno, Vice President, Front Range Community College, Larimer Campus, Ft. Collins, CO; Gary Hayter, Human Resources Specialist, Poudre School District R-1, Ft. Collins, CO; David Benson, EdD, Principal, Olander Elementary School, Ft. Collins, CO; Sue Minalta, Office Manager, Lincoln Junior High School, Ft. Collins, CO; Kathy Christie, Information Specialist, Education Commission of the States, Denver, CO: Dr. Helen Hartel, New York State Department of Education; Jewell Gould, American Federation of Teachers; Virginia Sargent, Recruiting Teachers, Belmont, MA; National Center for Education Information in New York; National Education Association, Washington, DC. I'd also like to thank my friend Martin Perlman for graciously giving me morale support.

K.M.

Contents

Contents

1

The Professional Resume

Whether you are on your way to becoming a teacher, administrator, career counselor, or media specialist, you will find education to be a rewarding profession. Many educators take a tremendous amount of pride in themselves and their work. While preparing your resume, keep in mind that this is not the time to be humble. This is where you get credit where credit's due.

A resume is something you should have in your back pocket, ready to give out at a moment's notice. Why? Because you'll never know when that special job opportunity may open up for you. Your resume is a custom-designed, self-marketing tool tailored to your career objectives. A professional resume functions in four ways:

1. It focuses the interviewer's attention on your strongest points.
2. It gives you full credit for all your achievements, whether you were paid or not.
3. It guides the interviewer toward positive things to talk about in discussing your credentials and focuses on the direction you want to go.
4. Most importantly, it lets you see yourself in a more focused and positive manner so that you can take control of your own future.

It's also the first link between you and the potential employer. (No wonder there's so much pressure on job seekers to create an effective resume.) To compete in today's job market, candidates need a good resume more than ever before. There are more people seeking work in the field of education than there are jobs available, especially for teaching positions.

Many of the resumes in this book are from actual educational professionals who have been clients of Just Resumes®. Others were created for this book with accurate job descriptions and educational requirements. These resumes provide examples of the kind of resume you—with the help of this book—are going to create. A number of these clients came to me with skills and education similar to yours. Working with them, I was able to produce a personalized resume that genuinely reflected their needs, accomplishments, and goals.

Before you tackle the resume writing process, please review my approach to creating a professional resume by reading this chapter and Chapter 2 ("The No-Nonsense Approach to Resume Writing"). At this point, you might be tempted to jump into writing your resume, but take a few additional minutes to read any of the next group of chapters that might apply to you. In Chapter 3, you'll find information on changing careers or making a lateral move. Chapter 4 shows you how to move up in the field you are in. And Chapter 5 offers suggestions for students and recent graduates. If you haven't done so already, next turn to the resume samples in Chapter 10 to see how all the theory behind resume writing has been turned into fact.

Reading the introductory chapters and surveying actual resumes will prime you for writing your own resume. You will also want to begin analyzing your own background and pinpointing your targeted career. What you have done in previous positions or gained through education and what you want to do in your career will also influence the resume format you choose. You might go with the traditional chronological format in which you highlight your jobs. You may wish to emphasize your skills by using the highly flexible functional format. Or you may opt to combine the chronological and functional formats, which allows you to highlight a specific job while also indicating other previous jobs. My step-by-step instructions and examples will prompt and guide you. Whichever format you decide to use, keep in mind that your aim is to capture your strongest qualities and focus them on your new job objective. Your professional style resume will show the interviewer and/or potential employer you are qualified for that desired position.

When you have completed your first draft, review this book's first two chapters, compare what you've written with the resumes I've included, and revise your work as necessary.

If your previous efforts to prepare a resume have been more frustrating than fun, believe me, you are not alone. Perhaps under a looming job interview deadline, you tried to put something together only to have the resume turn out flat and uninviting or scattered and unfocused.

Tip: Lack of focus on a future job objective is the number one reason most resumes fail. All too often, people begin a resume with the wrong focus and either are unable to complete it or else end up with an unsatisfactory product.

I ask my clients at Just Resumes® to concentrate on *where* they are going, rather than where they have been or where they are now. If you follow that approach, the resume will make use of your experience in a way that amplifies and directs those skills and experiences toward your goal. By focusing on the future job objective, you can create a resume that not only points you in the right direction but also shows the potential employer how the past and present qualify you for that job.

TIP FOR ELEMENTARY AND SECONDARY SCHOOL TEACHERS

Tip: Remember, interpersonal communication, knowledge, and educational background are all equally important skills to highlight on the resume.

TIPS FOR VOCATIONAL, COMMUNITY, AND JUNIOR COLLEGE INSTRUCTORS

Tip 1   The *Chronicle for Higher Education* is the primary source of information nationwide for vocational, community, and junior college positions.

Tip 2   Become familiar with the philosophy of the school district you are interested in working for. They are looking for teachers with the same philosophical views.

Tip 3   To teach noncredit classes in a vocational school, you need to document your area of expertise and/or certification. It is not necessary to have a degree to obtain a position in most vocational schools.

TIP FOR COLLEGE STUDENT TEACHERS

Tip: A great way to get interviews and network with the educational system is to go to the National Conference of your teaching area of interest. Ask your school advisor or career counselor where and when it will be held.

TIPS FOR ADMINISTRATORS, CAREER COUNSELORS, AND MEDIA SPECIALISTS

Tip 1   Membership in professional organizations and community service are very important for educational administrators and should be mentioned on the resume. Remember, you are the representative of the institution for the entire community.

Tip 2   To be an academic administrator, in most cases, you need to have a pattern of training and expertise in education. This includes classroom experience.

Tip 3   The cover letter has become increasingly important for academic administrators because it deals with specific issues used in the interviewing screening process.

TIPS FOR ALL EDUCATIONAL PROFESSIONAL JOB SEEKERS

This may be hard to believe, but many job applications live or die in the first 30 seconds of the screening process. It's in that 30-second glance that the receptionist or applications examiner decides either to forward your resume to the next step or to reject it. There are, however, several strategies you can use to increase your chances of having your resume reviewed by the interviewer.

Tip 1   Keep your resume to one or two pages. You'll notice that almost all the resume samples in this book are one page in length. If your resume is concise and to the point, it will emphasize the information that can convey your abilities and strengths. Of course, if you have so much experience that one page will not suffice, it is much better to use two pages than to try the faulty approach of cramming all the data onto one page by using a smaller and smaller typeface. You don't want to make the employer's job any tougher than it is by handing in a hard-to-read resume.

Tip 2   Your educational background always goes at the beginning of the resume when you apply for work at an educational institution.

Tip 3   State an objective. I advise clients to have an objective on their resumes, even a general objective. Faced with dozens of applications each day, the receptionist or human resources person doing the initial screening job does not want to take the time to determine what position you're applying for at the school or college. You'll also look more focused, and in turn more desirable for the position, than those whose resumes lack the objective. Their loss is your gain.

RESUME CHARACTERISTICS

As I mentioned earlier, there are three basic resume formats: the chronological, the functional, and the combination. The chronological emphasizes your jobs and is written in reverse chronological order. The functional style highlights your skills and places less emphasis on the job titles. A combination style makes use of the strengths of both the chronological and the functional formats.

Most of you will already be familiar with the traditional chronological format. Just remember that the functional, chronological, and combination resumes should offer the same information; the difference is in how the information is presented, in what is emphasized.

PERSONAL DATA

With today's equal opportunity requirements, personal data is not required, indeed does not belong, on a resume. I'll tell you a trade secret. Personnel agencies have admitted to me that they've seen examples of prejudice from the persons screening resumes. At times, the screener may not even be aware of this underlying bias.

SUMMARY OF RESUME STYLES

▶ The chronological format highlights the progress you've made in your jobs.
▶ The functional format highlights your skills.
▶ The combination format combines the chronological and functional formats to highlight selected jobs.

THE RESUME APPEARANCE: READY, GET SET, TYPE

The typeface you select is almost as important as the format you use for your resume. And with today's ever expanding computer typefaces, the choices can be overwhelming. To simplify the matter, opt for something that looks professional and is easy to read. A good typeface should enhance but not dominate your overall resume presentation (see samples in Chapter 10). Avoid the temptation to use a fancy script; more effective are such tested stalwarts as Helvetica, Century Schoolbook, or Univers, which are all available through laser printing and desktop publishing on both the Macintosh and IBM computer systems. The typesize should be no smaller than 11 point.

Don't scrimp when it comes to selecting your resume paper. Color and texture are the important factors in this area. For the educational professional, a brilliant white conveys a sense of competence. Ivory and light grey work well too. And, whether you're a teacher or administrator, your personal preference plays a part in this, too.

Many different textured papers are available. Parchment, for example, has a light textured background woven into the paper. Classic Laid, which is great for resumes, has a heavy, smooth, woodlike finish. Classic Linen has a lighter clothlike texture, and cotton, the most expensive, feels and looks just like cotton.

As with the typeface you choose, the resume paper should complement your resume, *not* dominate it. Resume paper and matching envelopes are available at your local copy shop.

RESUME DO'S AND DON'T'S

- ► DO choose a job that you "love."
- ► DO list all your good qualities. This is where you get credit where credit's due.
- ► DO include a clear and concise job objective; focus your resume on your objective to show the employer how the past and present qualify you for that job.
- ► DO include experience directly related to the objective.
- ► DO start each sentence with a vigorous action word.
- ► DO list all related experience, paid or unpaid if you're a recent graduate or are reentering the workforce. Include experience from community service, internships, and/or volunteer work.
- ► DO research the position and organization before the interview.
- ► DO keep your resume down to one or two pages.

▶ DO follow up the interview with a personalized thank-you letter.

▶ DON'T leave out the job objective.

▶ DON'T include material or history not related to the job objective.

▶ DON'T use long, repetitive explanations.

▶ DON'T include personal history.

▶ DON'T presume that the "personnel screener" understands skills included in the job title—tailor your job description.

▶ DON'T take for granted skills that you perform well as a matter of course.

▶ DON'T replace a job description with a job title—it's not self-explanatory. A teacher in one district may not have the same responsibilities as a teacher at another district.

▶ DON'T forget to include your GPA under education, if you're a student or recent graduate and it's 3.5 or higher.

▶ DON'T list references from whom you have not received permission or a positive response.

▶ DON'T send a "form" thank-you letter. Personalize each one.

▶ DON'T BE AFRAID TO SHOW OFF YOUR SKILLS.

2

The No-Nonsense Approach to Resume Writing

In a professionally designed resume, you can convey a significant amount of information concisely and vigorously. Straightforward, single-line phrases and sentences are easy to read, and direct the employer's attention toward your capabilities and desired experiences. If you prefer paragraph form, that style can be quite effective, though I find one-liners are more easily noticed and understood. Action words energize your resume, so in either case, begin each sentence with an action word, such as "implemented" or "designed," to describe what you do (see "More than 100 Action Words," at the end of this chapter).

REMEMBER: ALWAYS THINK POSITIVE AND FOCUS THE RESUME ON YOUR JOB OBJECTIVE.

THE BASIC RESUME ELEMENTS

Whether you decide to use the chronological, functional, or combination format will depend on the way you want to present your information. Your own background and your objective will determine which style will work best for you. No matter what the format, however, each resume should offer the same basic information:

- ▶ Name, address, and phone number.
- ▶ Career objective.
- ▶ Education, credentials, and/or certifications.
- ▶ Professional profile (optional).
- ▶ Community service.
- ▶ Affiliations.
- ▶ Description of work experience.
- ▶ Employment history with job title, organization name, location, and dates of employment.

Remember:

- ▶ All sentences start with a vigorous action verb.
- ▶ All job descriptions and experiences focus on the career objective.
- ▶ Education is placed before professional experience whenever you are applying for a position with an educational institution.

PREPARING THE CHRONOLOGICAL RESUME, STEP BY STEP

In the traditional chronological resume, you combine the experience and the employment history under one section. Each position is listed with the dates of employment, job title, organization name, city and state, followed by a point-by-point description of job experience. Jobs are listed in reverse order beginning with the most recent position.

The chronological resume highlights the progress in your jobs. Because of this, it works best for professionals who are making an upward career move in the educational profession.

As an example, let's say you are an English Instructor and you want to become the Dean of Instruction. In most cases, your goal would be this job progression: English Department Head; Assistant or Associate Dean; Dean of Instruction.

Tip 1 To move up in higher education, you need to demonstrate an increasing amount of leadership skills through your jobs, professional organizations, and community service.

Tip 2 There are more job opportunities in larger institutions than in smaller schools. (Although at smaller schools, you might be given more responsibilities.)

Use the chronological resume format when the following three points apply to you:

1. Your entire employment history shows progress with skills related to your objective. (Let's say you began your career as a teacher for an elementary school and you worked your way up to assistant principal and principal.)
2. Each position involves a generally different job description. (Looking at the preceding example, each position—from teacher to administrator (principal)—incorporates more responsibility and different job descriptions. The teacher instructs students in the classroom under the supervision of the principal. The principal administers all the teachers' classroom activities.)
3. Your work history is stable.

If these points reflect your job history, and you are aiming for a position that seems to follow from what you've previously been doing, then create a chronological resume by following these instructions:

1. List your name, address, and phone number. (College students: If you have a campus address and a permanent address, include both.)
2. Objective.
   What's your current objective? Make it brief and to the point, for example, "Media Specialist."
3. Education.
   Degree (BA, MA), major, school, graduation date. When you become certified, make sure to include this information here. Credentials can also appear here or have their own section.
4. Credentials.
   What are your state credentials and what is your specific area(s) of expertise? Do you have a lifetime credential?
5. Professional profile.
   This is a brief description or summary of your skills, personality traits, and achievements related to the job objective. What are personality traits? These are your particular characteristics that demonstrate your talents and abilities on the job. For example, let's say you want to be a Career Counselor. The interviewer(s) or committee will look for someone

who possesses excellent written and oral communication skills, and demonstrates understanding and empathy necessary for working with students.

6. Professional experience or related experience.

What date (year starting/ending) did you start your present job? What organization (name, city, and state) do you presently work for? For each job describe your work responsibilities and activities. Include any special achievements you've accomplished, related to your objective. Always focus on your strongest points, directly related to your career objective. Be consistent and provide the same kind of information about each previous job position pertinent to your objective. The following example shows this approach. Study the resume samples in Chapter 10 for more details and variations on the Professional Experience theme.

PROFESSIONAL EXPERIENCE

ART TEACHER (K–8) 1989-94

Bartlett Private Elementary School, Phoenix, AZ

- Established an art program and taught techniques and elements of design.
- Developed and implemented activities based on respect and enjoyment of the student's creativity, allowing originality through experimentation and manipulation of materials.
- Planned a variety of projects with a balance between two- and three-dimensional work, using traditional and unique materials.
- Provided classroom experiences, such as nonverbal instruction, nonverbal student interaction, and group activities.
- Emphasized problem solving and conceptual approaches.
- Introduced students to the history of art through films, slides, photographs, and guest speakers.
- Organized field trips to art museums, galleries, and studios.
- Participated in the production of children's musicals and plays.
  - Facilitated initial brainstorming sessions.
  - Designed and constructed sets, props, and costumes.
  - Worked with lighting and special effects; choreographed dance pieces.

PREPARING THE FUNCTIONAL RESUME, STEP BY STEP

For a functional resume, you will create subsections. The title of each subsection will depend on the skills you are highlighting as you aim toward your career objective. Teachers may use the actual courses taught as subsection titles. Then, describe each course and methods taught (see samples, Chapter 10).

Even with a quick glance, you can see that a functional resume looks different from a chronological resume. The functional format, because it highlights your skills, devotes a great deal more space to describing your experience. Such sections might include classroom or teaching experience, administration, and management to name a few. In breaking down the subsections in the functional resume by courses taught, teachers can follow the format shown in the following example:

PROFESSIONAL EXPERIENCE

FAMILY STUDIES TEACHER   1974-present

Pittsburgh High School, Pittsburgh, PA

- Teach Consumer and Family Studies to students in Grades 10–12.

Contemporary Living

- Teach students how to live independently.
- Discuss eating for good health, budgeting, banking, managing work and home.

Sociology of the Family

- Teach students how to understand themselves and families better.
- Discuss Individual Development, Dating, Sexuality, Media Influence, and Adulthood.

The actual employment history will be listed at the end of the resume and will concisely give the basic information as to job title, locations, and dates.

So, the functional resume uses the following format:

▶ All the work experience is highlighted by creating subsections pertinent to the job objective.

▶ The entire employment history appears at the end with job title, school district or institution name, city, state, and dates of employment; each job is listed in reverse chronological order, but without a detailed explanation of the experience.

If you are changing careers, seeking a job for the first time, or reentering the job market, the functional resume works best. (Does the following information sound similar to your own background?)

1. Your entire work history goes beyond the skills and experience related to your objective.
2. You have skills related to your job objective but not necessarily in your employment history.
3. You've had several positions with the same job description.

A functional resume is designed to be selective. If your entire work history includes additional skills not related to your career objective, you'll only highlight those skills pertinent to your objective.

If you've had several positions with the same job description, you don't need to repeat yourself. You'll only say what you did one time, which saves both space on the resume for other valuable information and time for the resume examiner. Don't worry that you might be minimizing your achievements, because you will list the jobs that cover similar experience under Employment History (see functional resume samples, Chapter 10). As you become familiar with the functional resume, you'll see how it can convey a great deal of information in a minimum amount of space. Now, follow these instructions:

1. List your name, address, and phone number. (College students: If you have a campus address and a permanent address, include both.)
2. Objective.
   What is your current objective? Make it brief and to the point, for example, "Media Specialist position."
3. Education.
   Degree (BA, MA), major, school, graduation date. If you're certified, make sure to include this information here.
4. Credentials.
   Your state credentials and specific area of expertise go here. Do you have a lifetime credential?
5. Professional profile.
   This is optional but useful. It's this section that my clients often refer to when they say "I can't believe this is me!" or "I

hadn't thought about myself before in this light!" This advice applies especially to educational professionals—you seem a bit coy about putting all your wonderful working traits on paper. Do it. It will show the employer that you are aware of your assets. Your profile is a brief description or summary of working style, personality traits, and achievements that relate to your objective. These are the essence of what the employer may be looking for in the applicant. You might write, for example, "Work well in a competitive and challenging environment." The resume samples in Chapter 10 will give you additional ideas for creating your Professional Profile.

6. Professional experience or related experience.

Here's the heart of your functional resume. Starting with the appropriate action word, describe what you do at your job. You'll use subheads to really convey your skills (see "More than 100 Action Words" at the end of this chapter). Part of the section would look like this:

PROFESSIONAL EXPERIENCE

Essential Skills Instructor

- Assessed students' individualized reading and writing skills and needs.
- Directed instruction in reading and writing skills.
- Supervised students in the reading lab.
- Directed and supervised instructional aide's work in classroom and office.
- Evaluated students' progress.

Education Coordinator

- Supervised and evaluated teachers and instructional aides.
- Coordinated student intake, assessment, and class placement.
- Monitored and evaluated instructional program and curriculum guidelines.
- Developed and facilitated staff in-service.
- Reported to Board of Directors on education program implementation and new program development.
- Interfaced and consulted with public agencies.
- Facilitated transition and served as liaison between administrators.

Remember to include any special achievements directly related to your career objective. Always focus on your strongest points that tie in to your career objective. For more details and examples, refer to the functional resume samples in Chapter 10.

7. Employment history.

In this section, list your job title, school district or institution name, city, state, and date position started/ended, starting with the most recent and working backward. Students and volunteers returning to the workforce may not have a job title. If your job title is nondescript or nonexistent, give yourself credit where credit is due. Be descriptive: When selecting an appropriate job title that best encapsulates what you do, remember that different school districts may have a different title for what is essentially the same job. For example, you might be called a Human Resources Assistant where you work, but your job may include more managerial duties than the title implies. Another school district might call that same position Assistant Director of Human Resources.

ORGANIZING THE EXPERIENCE SECTION IN A FUNCTIONAL RESUME

What you write in one part of the resume can help you flesh out other sections. This is especially the case for the Professional Experience section. To gain a better perspective, first list your Employment or Work History (which will appear at the end of your resume) before becoming more specific in describing your experience.

What you include under the Professional Experience heading essentially will be a description of your achievements and what you've done, taken directly from the Employment or Work History section. Remember, always focus the entire experience section on your career objective.

At this stage, you can afford to be expansive. Brainstorm your ideas. There really is no limit to the categories you can create. Start with an action word describing your experiences. After you've listed your achievements and experiences directly related to your career objective, sort out what you wrote. Then, create the subtitles that fit the description of your career objective and categorize the experiences by listing them under the appropriate subheading.

For example, let's say you're a soon-to-be-teacher graduate and have financed your education by working as a tutor and an instructor/counselor at a summer wheelchair sports camp. You've probably gained valuable experience and skills in teaching and communication. These very labels can become the categories that you will describe in detail under Professional Experience.

With this procedure, you're accomplishing two things. First, you're putting in concrete form a description of the many (and often unstated) ways you work. Second, you're highlighting the skills the interviewer will be looking for in you.

Now that you have those skills and/or areas of expertise listed as categories under Professional Experience, you can then use them as subheadings. If, as in the preceding example, you have a subheading for tutor or counselor, you now add the details of what that role involves:

Teaching Skills

- Tutor math, biology, physics, general and organic chemistry to college students on a one-on-one basis as well as in small group sessions.
  - Deal effectively with students of all levels and learning abilities.
  - Developed strong ability to present subject matter in multiple context tailored to individual needs.
  - Possess outstanding ability to motivate uninterested individuals in required nonmajor subjects.
- Taught private and public swim lessons to children and adults.
  - Instructed individuals and groups from beginners to competitive levels.

Communication Skills

- Conducted educational presentation to groups of 25–150 elementary, junior, and high school students throughout the community.
  - Provided awareness concerning relationships with a disabled person in the community through personal experience.
- Counsel and instruct disabled children and adolescents at the Lincoln County Junior Wheelchair Sports Camp.
  - Effectively motivate campers to learn new activities including: tennis . . . basketball . . . swimming . . . track and field . . . weight lifting . . . archery.
  - Provide continued support as a role model to handle real-life situations in a positive, calm, and diplomatic manner.

As you create your functional resume, visualize the employer receiving your final version. Remember, you're aiming for that interview; keep your resume on that target; keep your achievements and experience related to your career objective.

PREPARING THE COMBINATION RESUME, STEP BY STEP

By combining features of the chronological and functional resume, the combination resume allows the job seeker to highlight a specific job or selected jobs and still list other work experience or employment history. Let's say you are seeking a new position as a Career Counselor in the secondary school system. Your most recent position was as a High School Career Counselor. Previously, you have held jobs as a career counselor and also as an elementary school teacher. The most concise way for you to demonstrate your secondary school career counseling skills is to highlight your most recent job as Career Counselor and simply list your previous jobs. This format works well for those with the following background:

1. You've had specific job(s) directly related to your objective.
2. Each position involves a completely different job description.
3. You also have had related jobs that are important to mention because they are indirectly related to your current objective.
4. If you're a student, points one and two apply to your background, and you have jobs you'd like to mention just to show your stable work history.

For some of you, certain jobs you've had deserve more emphasis than others. A combination resume focuses on the jobs most directly related to your career objective.

A variation on the chronological and functional formats, the combination resume highlights the jobs that tie in to your objective by using the chronological style. Then it lists your other employment in the functional format. The combination format has an extensive job description for a specific job or jobs and then, in a different section, lists your previous employment history.

To create a combination resume, begin by following the same instructions for the chronological resume. This time, however, you'll highlight selected job(s) under the professional experience section that relate directly to your job objective (see instructions 1–5, in the section "Preparing the Chronological Resume, Step by Step"). In addition, you will also create a section for your previous jobs titled

Employment History and list them at the end of your resume. List your job title, organization name, city, state, and date position started/ended for the rest of your jobs in chronological order starting with the most recent and working backward as in the functional resume (see resume samples in Chapter 10).

NOTE: IF YOU'VE HAD NUMEROUS JOBS OVER THE YEARS, YOU DON'T *HAVE* TO LIST THEM ALL.

OPTIONAL RESUME HEADINGS

All resumes incorporate some flexibility. You may list some of the following skills or activities under the Professional Profile section or create titles for anything that's pertinent to your career objective and is important to you, such as:

Presentations	Publications
Public Speaking	Volunteer Work
Special Training	Academic Achievements
Certification	Affiliations
Community Service	Leadership Skills
Computer Hardware/Software	Other Pertinent Information
Computer Language Skills	Foreign Language Skills

MORE THAN 100 ACTION WORDS

act as	communicate	develop
active in	compute	direct
administer	conceptualize	distribute
allocate	consolidate	document
analyze	consult	draft
approve	contribute	edit
articulate	control	effect
assimilate	coordinate	enact
assist	correct	establish
assure	correspond	evaluate
augment	counsel	examine
balance	create	execute
built	delegate	follow up
chair	demonstrate	forecast
coach	design	formulate
collect	determine	forward

function	monitor	research
generate	motivate	resolve
guided	operate	restructure
identify	optimize	review
implement	organize	revise
improve	oversee	schedule
initiate	perform	screen
install	persuade	secure
institute	plan	select
instruct	prepare	serve
integrate	present	set up
interface	process	specify
interpret	produce	stimulate
interview	promote	strengthen
launch	proofread	summarize
lead	propose	supervise
lecture	provide	supply
liaison	recommend	systematize
locate	recruit	tabulate
maintain	refer	test
manage	repair	train
market	report	upgrade
mediate	represent	

3

Educational Professionals Making a Lateral Career Change or Changing Careers

MAKING A LATERAL MOVE

If you are making a lateral move to another school or department but essentially staying in the same field, use the functional style, which will emphasize your job skills (see Chapter 2).

In all cases, remember to focus on your career objective. Highlight all the training you received and the duties you're currently responsible for.

CHANGING CAREERS

In the past, employees tended to stay with one employer for long periods, even for whole careers. People also remained in the same field for the most part. But now, it is not at all unusual for many of us to begin in our twenties in one field, move to another area of work in our thirties, and again switch gears in our forties. A former Nursing Instructor, for example, may take a position as Nursing Educator for a hospital.

This fluidity of professional development calls for the functional resume because you are going to be focusing on your skills, not just your employment history. You may be a Publicity Director aiming for a change as a Director of Public Information, and embedded in your past are skills and strengths, such as your ability to make contacts in the community, that apply to that new career objective.

Using a functional resume format, you'll create the heading of Related Experience. Under that heading, you can display your skills, as in the following example:

Publicity Writer

- Develop, write, and edit on the Macintosh computer promotional material and advertising copy using information from artists, agents, and personal research.
  - Promotional pieces and ads are aimed at the public, students, faculty, and staff.
  - Events include concerts and recitals by classical, jazz, folk, and contemporary music artists; theater; ballet, modern, and ethnic dance; a series of family events; artist lecture/ demonstrations; and lectures by public figures in the arts, science, and public affairs.
- Work closely with Marketing Director and staff graphic artist to budget schedule and prepare press releases, seasonal quarterly brochures, annual brochure, posters, fliers, advertising, direct mail, promotional articles, subscription letters, and displays.
- Proof all copy.
- Update and maintain promotion files.
- Participate in weekly staff meetings, join in special department projects, and lend a helping hand during staff shortages.
- Hire, train, and supervise marketing copywriter interns.

Outside College Representative

- Develop and maintain direct relationships with local newspaper, radio, and television news media, arts writers, critics, and editors; identify and cultivate new audience markets and seek underrepresented constituencies.
- Serve as liaison between artists and media for interviews and feature story profiles.
- Tape voice-overs and serve as program spokeperson to promote events through local media.

What can often lead to a career change is the discovery that you make about yourself when you pursue a new hobby, take a class, or help a friend or family member on a special project. These activities represent more than "hidden" skills; they are true indicators of your interest that translate so well into the essence of a functional resume.

Tip: To become a professor at a four-year university, you must have a PhD. With a Master's degree you may become a part-time instructor at a four-year university or at a community college system. Those who don't have the required degrees may teach in a private or vocational college setting.

RETURNING TO THE WORKFORCE

Many women return to the teaching workforce after taking valuable time off to raise a family or engage in other occupations. If you're interested in returning to a teaching position, it's important to be aware of the philosophy of the school district you'd like to work for.

Tip: You must keep current with the latest in educational technology. You can do this by taking classes, working as a classroom volunteer, and serving on committees in your local community to demonstrate leadership skills.

Again, the functional resume will best highlight your specialized skills to show the potential employer how well your past and present qualify you for that new career (see Chapter 2, "Preparing the Functional Resume").

For those of you who have related volunteer experience but didn't have a job title, be descriptive. Give yourself a job title that describes what you did. For example, if you were a volunteer for the PTA who performed the duties of Social Chair, give yourself the job title of Social Chair or Volunteer Social Chair.

TEACHING TRENDS IN THE 1990s FOR ELEMENTARY AND SECONDARY TEACHERS

Teaching trends for K–12 teachers for the 1990s involve moving toward site-based management and away from centralized governance.

Another trend in education is integration of technology and learning; for example, teachers now may apply reading and writing skills in other areas such as social studies, math, and/or science studies.

Flexible grouping of children is also a trend for the 1990s; for example, integrating challenged youngsters or having some children stay with the same teacher two consecutive years, especially for a specific subject such as science or math.

4

The Educational Professional Moving Up

The educational profession is a fast-growing and ever-demanding field. Once you get your degree and pass the certified board exams, there is a great demand for educational professionals. Not only are there shortages of some positions, there are also new positions opening up every year. You might be a teacher, administrator, career counselor, or media specialist; and at some point, whether by necessity or choice, you are ready to advance to a higher position. Regardless of the business climate—whether we're in the midst of a recession or a booming economy—an effective resume can help you reposition yourself.

You need a way of highlighting your progress and achievements in a resume that will not only be competitive but will get results. You want to show potential employers that you are thinking in terms of a career and not just a job.

Tip: Those teachers wanting to move into administration need to demonstrate strong leadership skills; for example, serve on the Site-Based, Decision-Making Committee; Curricular Committee; School Goal or Staff Development Committee; and/or district level committees, such as Curricular Adoption Committee or Task Forces, or Study Committee.

The committees you have served on become very important information to highlight in your resume. If you are not advancing as quickly as you think you deserve to, a professional resume emphasizing your work history can offer you the psychological boost you need to present yourself in the best possible light. Not only will your resume show employers your capabilities, it will also show *you* what you have done, so you can proceed in a positive and focused manner toward that goal.

Tip: Whether you are a teacher moving up to department head or assistant dean moving to dean of instruction, I recommend the chronological resume format, which will best highlight the progress of your jobs and skills.

5

Resumes for the Educational Student and Recent Graduate

You can study hard in school for four years, graduate with honors, and yet, when it comes time to enter the job market, the first request the interviewer makes is "to see a copy of your resume."

A good resume that represents your hard-earned skills and accomplishments will help you bridge the gap between college and the work world.

Tip 1   Students, too, may volunteer on school district committees. By doing so, you will stand out from your peers. In addition, you will be able to increase your networking with the school districts as well as demonstrate leadership skills that are so important to your profession.

Tip 2   National conferences in your teaching area are a great way to schedule interviews and network with the educational community. Check with your career advisor or counselor for more information in your local area.

A large percentage of campus recruits from school districts nationwide will offer a teacher's job fair. These job fairs are well worth going to. They are a great resource for networking as well as landing a teaching job.

Tip: There are five Regional Accrediting Agencies in the country that establish the minimum standards for college levels of teaching qualifications.

For the majority of college students, a functional resume highlighting skills is the ticket to getting that interview. Most college students do not have enough experience to warrant using a chronological resume. However, a student who has had several unrelated paid jobs and has also had internships and/or volunteer committee or other work experience can list those unpaid though valuable assets under Experience in the flexible combination resume.

Many college students are skilled in computers whether through college, on-the-job training, or personal experience.

Tip: Computer skills are a universal requirement among educational professionals. Keep up with the latest in technology and, again, get to know your district's teaching philosophy.

STUDENTS, GRADUATES, AND THE TWO-PAGE RESUME

As is the case for most professional resume writers, students and recent graduates should usually be able to create a one-page resume. But some graduates may have an abundance of related experience requiring a two-page resume. That is all right. I would rather you have a well-written and properly formatted two-page resume than a poorly written, crowded one-pager. Don't use a smaller typeface in hopes of getting all the information onto one page. Such a tactic will hinder rather than improve your job chances. No employer wants to bother with a hard-to-read resume.

Here are a couple of pointers for those of you with a two-page resume: Add the word "-More-" or "-Continued-" at the bottom of the first page and place your name and the words "Page Two" at the top of the second page.

COLLEGE GRADUATES ENTERING
THE PROFESSIONAL WORLD

Some college graduates have previous paid experience involving skills that directly relate to the jobs they're applying for. For example, let's say you had a part-time job during your last two years of college as a teaching assistant, and now, as a graduate, you are seeking a teaching position at another college. You would use the chronological format to detail job experiences that point toward your future position. The chronological resume format works best in this situation because it emphasizes the jobs you have held that directly lead toward your career objective.

WHAT IF YOU HAVE NO PAID EXPERIENCE?

Many college students do not have any paid job experience that ties into their job objective. That might seem like an insurmountable barrier, for as we all know, many organizations won't hire someone until he or she has experience in the field. But how do you obtain experience if no one will hire you?

Well, don't give up. I've found that most of my clients, even students, have some sort of related experience to write about in their resume for that upcoming job or they wouldn't be interested in applying for it.

Think back over your school years. Perhaps you worked on school projects related to your job objective. Or what about those committees you've been on as an active member? And don't forget volunteer work and/or internships in your field as well as any special achievements that are directly related to your career objective.

In a functional style, here's how I would arrange the resume for a fourth-year student with student teaching experience, who has not yet received his/her teaching credential but wants to find a part-time student teacher or teaching assistant position with a secondary school.

Under Objective, we would write:

Student Teacher position

Under Education we would write:

BA Degree, Education, 1995
University of California, Santa Barbara, CA
Education GPA: 3.53

We would also list related classes taken under the Education heading.

Under Related Experience, we would create the following appropriate subheading:

Classroom Experience

- Assisted teacher with instruction of third-grade students in daily classroom activities in all areas of the curriculum.
- Worked with children in group sessions and one-on-one.
- Concerned with the total growth and needs of the child involving social, emotional, intellectual, creative, and physical behavior.

- Built child's self-esteem and self-confidence. Effectively motivated children to maximize participation and enjoyment.
- Supervised children on field trips.

As you can see, you certainly don't have to have paid job experience to apply this method to your situation. Through school projects and committee experience, you can demonstrate to your potential employers that you have the experience to move into paid employment. By the way, committee experience demonstrates great leadership skills, a quality that all the school districts look for in their on-campus recruiting.

For those of you with internship experience and unrelated previous employment (fast foods, sales clerk, etc.), I recommend the combination resume format (see Chapter 2). Basically, you will highlight your internship or selected job(s) in a chronological format under the Related Experience heading and place your other jobs under Employment History at the bottom of the resume, as in the functional format.

This method helps to solve the Catch-22 problem in which an organization won't hire you unless you have experience and it seems impossible to gain experience unless you get hired. By pinpointing your projects and volunteer work, you can demonstrate to employers and to yourself that you have what it takes to obtain that valued first job!

THE FIRST-YEAR STUDENT VERSUS THE RECENT COLLEGE GRADUATE

Most soon-to-be graduates are seeking *full-time* work. But what if you're a first- or second-year student seeking a *part-time* employment or internship in your field of study? Go for it! The key word here is *part-time*. To some employers, a first-year student means stability. Employers feel there's a good chance students will plan on staying with the organization or school district throughout their school years. That could mean 2 to 4 years of employment for you.

For additional ideas and examples, see the college student and recent graduate resume samples provided in Chapter 10. I have also provided a cover letter for a soon-to-be graduate in Chapter 6.

6

The Cover Letter and Thank-You Letter

ABOUT COVER LETTERS

Most resumes are not complete without a cover letter, which introduces you and your resume to the employer. Because the cover letter provides essential information not found in the resume, one is needed whenever you mail your resume to an employer. They can be personalized or generalized, but are written specifically to go with the individual's resume. You can create an effective cover letter in three paragraphs.

1. The first paragraph states why you are writing, that is, what position you're applying for and whether you saw an advertisement or heard about the position or company through a referral or by reputation.

2. The second paragraph is a brief summary stating why you feel qualified for the position. What makes you different? If adding the Professional Profile section in a resume will make an otherwise one-page resume into two pages, I'll use it in a cover letter instead. Never use it for both or repeat verbatim what is said in the resume, unless you're answering an ad that specifically requests information in the cover letter.

3. The third paragraph is the closing statement saying where you can be reached and thanking the employer.

The following sample cover letters demonstrate this format.

SAMPLE COVER LETTERS

January 2, 1995

David Benson, EdD
Principal
Olander Elementary School
3401 Auntie Stone Street
Fort Collins, CO 80526

Dear Dr. Benson:

I am applying for an elementary teaching position with your school district. My friend Scott Mullen, a teacher at Olander Elementary School, referred me to you for this position.

My dedication and enthusiasm for teaching children extends far beyond the classroom. I enjoy working with the parents to help improve their children's education, and I feel that involving the community in our educational system is important. I am confident I will make an excellent role model for your students and an important contribution to your staff and community.

Enclosed is my application and resume, which provides additional information about my education and professional experience. I may be reached at the address and phone number above. I will be glad to make myself available for an interview at your earliest convenience to discuss how my qualifications would be consistent with your needs. Thank you.

Sincerely,

Holly C. Jones

February 12, 1995

June Holmstrum, Principal
Shepardson Elementary School
115 East Elizabeth Street
Fort Collins, CO 80524

Dear June Holmstrum:

I'm seeking an entry level position leading to a teaching career with your school district. Being aware of your excellent reputation and firm commitment to the educational community of Fort Collins, I would like to express a sincere interest to be a part of your teaching staff.

I will be graduating from the University of California at Santa Barbara in June 1995. While financing my education with experience as a teacher's aide and volunteering as a student teacher, I continue to maintain a GPA of 3.59. I have excellent leadership skills, enthusiasm, and dependability with a strong desire to learn and excel. I am confident I will make a significant contribution to your staff now, and an increasingly important one in years to come.

Enclosed is my resume for more detailed information about my experience. I may be reached at the addresses and phone numbers above. I will be happy to make myself available for an interview at any time to discuss how my qualifications would be consistent with your needs. Thank you for your time and consideration.

Sincerely,

Ladd Jacobs

ABOUT THANK-YOU LETTERS

You send a thank-you letter after you've had an interview for a position you're interested in. The thank-you letter should be mailed the day of the interview; it should be brief and personalized. Follow this three-paragraph procedure:

1. In the opening paragraph, thank the interviewer and reemphasize your interest in the position.
2. The second paragraph reminds the employer why you are a good candidate for the position. Mention something specific from the interview.
3. The closing paragraph again says thanks and states that you look forward to hearing from the interviewer.

Sending a thank-you letter after the interview will reinforce in the interviewer's mind just how serious and enthusiastic you are about the position. That very act can separate you from the other applicants, giving you the extra something that leads to your being hired. The following sample thank-you letter shows the correct format.

SAMPLE THANK-YOU LETTER

January 3, 1995

Dear Mr. Charles:

Thank you for spending so much time with me yesterday. I am very excited about the prospect of seeking a teaching position with the Birmingham School District.

After spending the majority of my time working on a part-time basis as a teacher's aide, as well as volunteering as a student teacher and board member for several committees in our community, I am eager to start working full time. I thrive on working in a fast-paced and competitive environment.

I'm happy to say, we share the same philosophy in what it takes to offer quality education. Being aware of your excellent reputation and commitment to the educational community in Birmingham, I would be proud to be a member of your teaching staff.

If you have any questions, feel free to call me at any time.

Sincerely,

Brett Aronson

7

Job Trends to Look For in the 1990s

According to the U.S. Department of Labor Bureau of Labor Statistics *Occupational Outlook Handbook*, employment for teachers is expected to grow from 3,587,000 in 1991 to 3,954,000 by the year 2000. Other careers for the teaching profession include career or guidance counselors, librarians or media specialists, and college or school administrators, such as the principal, academic dean, and director of admissions.

The following sections provide a breakdown of the job outlook for teachers, counselors, and media specialists.

TEACHERS

Kindergarten and Elementary-School Teachers

Teachers for kindergarten and elementary schools held about 1,520,000 jobs in 1990. More than 8 out of 10 worked in public schools. Most were in schools that have students in kindergarten through grade six; however, some taught in middle schools, where students are between the upper elementary and lower high school grades. In addition, most of the 332,000 special education teachers taught in elementary schools.

All states and the District of Columbia require certification for teachers in public elementary schools. Usually, certification is granted by the state board of education through a certification advisory committee. Generally, however, requirements include a bachelor's degree and completion of an approved teacher training program with a prescribed number of education credits.

Employment of kindergarten and elementary school teachers is expected to grow about as fast as the average for all occupations through the year 2005 as enrollments increase and class size declines. The number of job openings for elementary school teachers should increase substantially from the mid-1990s to the year 2005 as the large number of teachers now in their forties and fifties reach retirement age.

Employment of special education teachers in elementary schools is expected to increase much faster than the average for all occupations through the year 2005 due to recent federal legislation emphasizing training and employment for individuals with disabilities; technological advances resulting in more survivors of accidents and illnesses; and growing public interest in individuals with special needs.

Related occupations include preschool workers, trainers, and employee development specialists, employment interviewers, education administrators, college and university faculty, media specialists, personnel specialists, public relations specialists, social workers, and counselors.

Secondary-School Teachers

Secondary-school teachers held about 1,280,000 jobs in 1990; more than 9 out of 10 were in public schools. In addition, some of the 332,000 special education teachers worked in secondary schools.

All 50 states and the District of Columbia require teachers in pubic secondary schools to be certified. Certification is generally for one or several related subjects. Usually, certification is granted by the state board of education or a certification advisory committee.

Requirements for regular certificates vary by state. All states however, require a bachelor's degree and completion of an approved teacher training program with a prescribed number of subject and education credits and supervised practice teaching in a secondary school.

Employment of secondary-school teachers is expected to increase faster than the average for all occupations through the year 2005 as high school enrollments grow and class size declines. Job openings for secondary-school teachers are expected to increase substantially by the end of the decade as the large number of teachers now in their forties and fifties reach retirement age.

Because of recent federal legislation, as previously mentioned, employment of special education teachers in high schools is expected to increase much faster than the average for all occupations through the year 2005.

Related occupations include school administrators, college faculty, counselors, trainers, and employee development specialists, employment interviewers, media specialists, public relations representatives, sales representatives, and social workers.

Adult Education Teachers

Adult education teachers held about 517,000 jobs in 1990. Almost half taught part time, a larger proportion than for other teachers, and many taught intermittently. Many adult education teachers are self-employed. Adult education teachers are employed by public school systems; community and junior colleges; universities; businesses that provide formal education and training for their employees; community organizations; business schools, and so on.

Training requirements vary widely by state and by subject. In general, teachers need work or other experience in their field, and a license or certificate in fields where these usually are required for full professional status.

Employment of adult education teachers is expected to grow faster than the average for all occupations through the year 2005 as the demand for adult education programs continues to rise. An increasing number of adults are taking courses for career advancement, skills upgrading, and personal enrichment.

Adult education teaching requires a wide variety of skills and aptitudes, including the power to influence, motivate, and train others; organizational, administrative, and communication skills; and creativity. Workers in related occupations that require these aptitudes include other teachers, counselors, school administrators, public relations specialists, employee development specialists and interviewers, and social workers.

College Faculty

College and university faculty held about 712,000 jobs in 1990, mostly in public institutions. About 3 out of 10 college and university faculty members work part time. Some part-timers, known as "adjunct faculty," have primary jobs outside of academia.

Employment of college faculty is expected to increase about as fast as the average for all occupations through the year 2005 as enrollments in higher education increase. Many additional openings will arise as faculty members retire.

College and university faculty function both as teachers and researchers. Related occupations for college and university faculty include elementary and secondary school teachers, media specialists, writers, consultants, lobbyists, trainers, and employee development specialists, and policy analysts. Faculty research activities are often similar to those of scientists, project managers, and administrators in industry, government, and nonprofit research organizations.

COUNSELORS

Counselors held about 144,000 jobs in 1990. School counseling was the largest specialty. In addition to working in elementary and secondary schools and colleges, however, counselors worked in a wide variety of public and private establishments.

Generally, counselors have a master's degree in college student affairs, elementary or secondary school counseling, gerontological counseling, marriage and family counseling, substance abuse counseling, mental health counseling, counseling psychology, career counseling, or related field.

Overall employment of counselors is expected to grow faster than the average for all occupations through the year 2005. In addition, replacement needs should increase significantly by the end of the decade as the large number of counselors now in their forties and fifties reach retirement age.

Employment of school counselors is expected to grow faster than average because of increasing secondary school enrollments, state legislation requiring counselors in elementary schools, and the expanded responsibilities of counselors. Counselors are increasingly becoming involved in crisis and preventive counseling, helping students deal with issues ranging from drug and alcohol abuse to death and suicide.

Related occupations include college and student personnel workers, teachers, personnel workers and managers, social workers, psychologists, psychiatrists, members of the clergy, occupational therapists, training and development specialists, and equal employment opportunity/affirmative action specialists.

MEDIA SPECIALISTS

Media specialists, formerly titled librarians, held about 149,000 jobs in 1990. Most were in school and academic libraries. A master's degree in library science (MLS) is necessary for media specialist positions in most academic and in some school libraries.

Graduates of MLS programs should have favorable job prospects largely due to the decline in the number of such graduates during the 1980s. Many job openings for media specialists will result from the need to replace those who retire, transfer to other occupations, or leave the labor force for other reasons.

Employment of media specialists is expected to grow more slowly than the average for all occupations through the year 2005.

Related occupations include archivists, information scientists, museum curators, publishers' representatives, research analysts, information brokers, and records managers.

8

Interviewing and Job Searching in the Educational Profession

Going on an interview can be both nerve-racking and exciting. Following these suggestions can greatly reduce your tension level:

1. Call the school district and ask for information. In the interview, when you are asked if you know about the school district, it is impressive to mention various aspects of their programs. A little bit of research can go a long way.

Tip: Know the school district's purpose and philosophy. Be prepared to let the interviewer(s) know you are aware of the district's needs and reputation. School administrators may be philosophically biased.

Before you interview, you can call or write the school district's human resources department to request this specific information.

Tip: Be prepared to interview with the principal, staff members, and parents, in some cases.

2. For out-of-town organizations, check with the reference librarian of your public library for more information about the school district or organization.

3. Bring three or four resumes with you to the interview. You could be interviewed by several decision makers. Hand a resume to each interviewer and always keep one for yourself. Chances are the interviewer will use your resume to interview you, and having it available will make the experience go a lot smoother for everyone. It's permissible to refer to your resume during the interview, though I suggest you try to memorize its main points beforehand.

4. Always bring a notepad and pen to the interview. Ask questions about the job and take notes. You may want to jot down a few questions before the interview. Also, remember to write the interviewer's name and title (with the correct spelling) on your notepad to address a thank-you letter after the interview.

Tip: It is impressive to most recruiters that you came prepared for the interview. It demonstrates to them just how serious you are about the job.

5. Remember, think positive! Focus on your strengths. Talk about what you do have to offer, not what you don't. If you're applying for a position you do not have experience in yet, focus on enthusiasm and eagerness to learn. Do not even think about your lack of experience. Enthusiasm is a great asset that employers notice. Sometimes, they would rather train an enthusiastic employee with no experience than hire an experienced employee who lacks that quality. We all know that most educational professionals already have gone through several years of specialized training. Many employers are seeking a trained professional for a specific position who has leadership skills. If you can demonstrate that you possess this quality in yourself, it is likely that you'll get the job.

6. The desire for job security is also something most employers like to hear about. It confirms in their minds that you really are planning to stay with the school district for a decent amount of time. But most importantly, it provides a bond that is mutually beneficial for both parties—employer and employee.

7. After the interview, immediately send a personalized thank-you letter to the potential employer.

TOUGH QUESTIONS MOST ASKED IN A TEACHER'S INTERVIEW

School districts, in general, look for candidates who demonstrate strong interpersonal communication skills, technical knowledge, appropriate educational background, and similar philosophical views.

Tip 1   When interviewing for a community or junior college, keep in mind that the hiring committee for teachers may be seeking a 30-year commitment. This is especially true for tenure or continuing contract positions. Elementary and secondary school districts want a 3–5-year commitment.

Tip 2   A current trend in education is to prepare a mini (15–30 minutes) lesson for the interview. So be prepared. Chances are they will let you know before the interview. If not, ask.

The following are the kind of questions you will most likely be asked in the interview:

1. How do you organize and deliver your instructional program?
2. How would you resolve a conflict? Tell me about one that didn't come out right. What did you learn from it?
3. If I (principal) talked to the children in your classroom, what would they say about their experience? If I spoke to the children's parents, what would they say?
4. What teaching skills are you working on to improve your effectiveness in the classroom?
5. What kind of principal do you want to work for?
6. What do you like least about the faculty lounge? This is a tricky question. (The answer they most look for is "gossip.")
7. What's is your vision of the perfect school? (Match the school's own values and philosophy.)

QUESTIONS FOR YOU TO ASK THE INTERVIEWER

1. What is the school district's philosophy? (Even if you've done your homework and are aware of their philosophy, if it hasn't come up yet, it is a question most principals like to be asked about.)

2. What do you expect from your teachers? (This is another good question to ask the interviewer(s).)
3. What kind of governance or decision making is modeled in the school?

LIST OF REFERENCES AND LETTERS OF RECOMMENDATION

Most employers will ask for three personal and/or business references. Simply list the name, professional title, and place of employment (with address and phone number) for each reference. Prior to using anyone's name as a reference, always let the contact know that you plan to do so and make sure the person will give you a *good* one. It's usually unnecessary to mail references with your resume and cover letter unless requested. It is, however, a good idea to bring them with you to the interview along with a letter of recommendation. A letter of recommendation is the letter written by a previous employer on the company stationery, highly recommending you for the position. If the letter doesn't provide such a testimonial, don't use it.

WHAT TO WEAR ON THE INTERVIEW

Always dress appropriately for an interview. Your appearance will be the interviewer's first impression of you. Women should wear a suit, conservative dress, or skirt, blouse, and blazer. Men should wear a suit and tie. Even if you know the organization's employees dress casually on the job, you are not an employee, yet. You want to look businesslike and professional. Dressing up for the interview shows the employer you take your work seriously. Believe me, it will make a difference.

TIPS ON JOB SEARCHING

Tip 1   If you know what school district you'd like to work for, check with the human resources office to learn how and where they advertise.

Tip 2   Some of the best places to contact for school district placement are the college placement services, offered by the state boards of education in individual school districts.

9

Alphabetical Listing of Associations and Publications for the Educational Profession

The following associations are listed alphabetically by category of interest or purpose (e.g., administration, literacy, science).

National Council for Accreditation of Teacher Education (NCATE)
2010 Massachusetts Avenue NW, Suite 200
Washington, DC 20036-1023
(202) 466-7496

Members: 556

Publications: *Annual List of Accredited Institutions; Directory of Nationally Accredited Schools of Teacher Education; Quality Teaching; Standards, Procedures, and Policies for the Accreditation of Professional Education Units; NCATE-Approved Curriculum Guidelines.*

American Association of School Administrators (Administration) (AASA)
1801 North Moore Street
Arlington, VA 22209
(703) 528-0700

Members: 18,000

Publications: *Leadership News; The School Administrator.*

American Federation of School Administrators (Administration) (AFSA)
1729 21st Street NW
Washington, DC 20009
(202) 986-4209

Members: 12,000

Publication: *AFSA News.*

Association of Governing Boards of Universities and Colleges (Administration) (AGB)
1 Dupont Circle NW, Suite 400
Washington, DC 20036
(202) 296-8400

Members: 32,000

Publications: *AGB Notes; AGB Reports.*

National FFA Organization (Agricultural Education) (NFFAO)
National FFA Center
Box 15160
5632 Mount Vernon Memorial Highway
Alexandria, VA 22309-0160
(703) 360-3600

Members: 385,376

Publications: *Between Issues; FFA Times; National FFA Organization—Update; National FFA Convention Proceedings; FFA New Horizons Magazine.*

National Art Education Association (Arts) (NAEA)
1916 Association Drive
Reston, VA 22091-1590
(703) 860-8000

Members: 13,000

Publications: *Art Education; NAEA Newsletter; Studies in Art Education.*

Intercultural Development Research Association (Bilingualism) (IDRA)
5835 Callaghan Road, Suite 350
San Antonio, TX 78228
(210) 684-8180

Nonmembership

Publications: *IDRA Newsletter; The Undereducation of American Youth; Hispanic Families as Valued Partners.*

National Association for Bilingual Education (Bilingualism) (NABE)
Union Center Plaza
810 First Street NE, Third Floor
Washington, DC 20002
(202) 898-1829

Members: 3,000

Publications: *Annual Conference Journal; Newsletter; Journal.*

National Association of Biology Teachers (NABT)
11250 Roger Bacon Drive, No. 19
Reston, VA 22090
(703) 471-1134

Members: 7,000

Publications: *American Biology Teacher; National Association of Biology Teachers—News and Views; Careers in Biology.*

Foundation for Student Communication (Business Education) (FSC)
305 Aaron Burr Hall
Princeton, NJ 08544-1011
(609) 258-1111

Members: 218,000

Publications: *Business Today: Published for Students by Students.*

Junior Achievement (Business Education)
1 Education Way
Colorado Springs, CO 80906
(719) 540-8000

Members: 1,200,000

Publications: *Junior Achievement Annual Report; PARTNERS.*

National Association of Classroom Educators in Business Education
(NACEBE)
Watauga High School
Highway 105 South
Boone, NC 28607
(704) 264-2407

Members: 700

Publications: *Directory of Officers and Committee Members; Newsletter.*

National Association of Supervisors of Business Education (NASBE)
Fort Worth Independent School District
3210 West Lancaster
Fort Worth, TX 76107
(817) 878-3741

Members: 300

Publications: *National Association of Supervisors of Business Education—Newsletter.*

National Association of Teacher Educators for Business Education (NATEBE)
University of Missouri-Columbia
Business Education Department
303 Hill Hall
Columbia, MO 65211
(314) 882-2377

Members: 350

Publication: *Newsletter.*

National Business Education Association (NBEA)
1914 Association Drive
Reston, VA 22091
(703) 860-8300

Members: 18,000

Publications: *Business Education Forum; Keying In.*

Association for Childhood Education International (ACEI)
11501 Georgia Avenue, Suite 312
Wheaton, MD 20902
(301) 942-2443

Members: 17,000

Publications: *ACEI Exchange; Childhood Education; Journal of Research in Childhood Education.*

National Association for the Education of Young Children (Childhood Education) (NAEYC)
1834 Connecticut Avenue NW
Washington, DC 20009
(202) 232-8777

Members: 75,000

Publications: *Early Childhood Research Quarterly; Young Children.*

National Elementary School Center (Childhood Education) (NESC)
2 East 103rd Street
New York, NY 10029
(212) 289-5929

Members: 200

Publications: *Conference Proceedings; FOCUS; The School as Locus of Advocacy for All Children; Focus on the Child.*

Parent Cooperative Pre-Schools International (Childhood Education) (PCPI)
PO Box 90410
Indianapolis, IN 46290
(317) 849-0992

Members: 12,500

Publications: *Cooperatively Speaking; PCPI Director; How to Start a Co-Op; Health and Safety in the Preschool; Leadership Development—A Facilitator's Handbook.*

World Organization for Early Childhood Education, United States National Committee
University of South Florida
1012 Sylvia Lane
Tampa, FL 33613
(813) 974-5755
Members: 400
Publications: *International Journal of Early Childhood; OMEP/USNC Directory; OMEP/USNC Newsletter.*

Chinese Language Teachers Association (CLTA)
Kalamazoo College
Foreign Languages
1200 Academy Street
Kalamazoo, MI 49006
(616) 337-7001

Members: 700

Publications: *CLTA Newsletter; Directory.*

Junior Classical League (Classical Studies-High School)
Miami University
Oxford, OH 45056
(513) 529-7741
Members: 50,000
Publication: *Torch.*

Pompeiiana, Inc. (Classical Studies) (PI)
6026 Indianola Avenue
Indianapolis, IN 46220
(317) 255-0589

Members: 6,000
Publication: *Pompeiiana Newsletter.*

American Association of Community and Junior Colleges (AACJC)
National Center for Higher Education
1 Dupont Circle NW, Suite 410
Washington, DC 20036-1176
(202) 728-0200

Members: 1,113

Publications: *AACJC Community, Technical, and Junior College Times; Who's Who in Community, Technical, and Junior Colleges; AAACJC Journal; AACJC Membership Directory; Statistical Yearbook of Community, Technical, and Junior Colleges.*

Association of Community College Trustees (Community Colleges) (ACCT)
740 North Street NW
Washington, DC 20036
(202) 775-4667

Members: 780

Publications: *ACCT; Advisor; Trustee Quarterly.*

League for Innovation in the Community College (Community Colleges)
25431 Cabot Road, Suite 204
Laguna Hills, CA 92653
(714) 855-0710

Members: 18

Publication: *Innovator.*

National Council for Research and Planning (Community Colleges) (NCRP)
Radford University
PO Box 6924
Radford, VA 24142
(703) 639-1263

Members: 256

Publications: *Community College Journal for Research and Planning; Community College Resource Review; Membership Directory; New Directions for Two-Year Colleges.*

National Council of State Directors of Community and Junior Colleges
Michigan Department of Education
PO Box 30008
Lansing, MI 48909
(517) 373-3360

Members: 38

Publications: Unknown

National Community Education Association (NCEA)
801 North Fairfax Street, Suite 209
Alexandria, VA 22314
(703) 683-6232

Members: 1,500

Publications: *Community Education Journal; Community Education Today.*

American Computer Science League (ACSL) (Secondary Schools)
PO Box 40118
Providence, RI 02940
(401) 331-ACSL

Participants: 600

Publication: *Newsletter.*

American Association for Adult and Continuing Education (AAACE)
2101 Wilson Boulevard, Suite 925
Arlington, VA 22201
(703) 522-2234

Members: 4,000

Publications: *Adult Education; Adult Learning Practitioner Journal; American Association for Adult and Continuing Education—Newsletter.*

Cooperative Work Experience Education Association (CWEEA)
Illinois State Board of Education
100 North First Street
Springfield, IL 62777
(217) 782-4862

Members: 1,300

Publications: *Cooperative Work Experience Education Association— Exchange Bulletin; Cooperative Work Experience Education Association— Membership Directory; Coordination; Coordination Experts.*

Future Problem Solving Program (Cooperative Learning) (FPSP)
315 West Huron, Suite 140 B
Ann Arbor, MI 48103-4203
(313) 998-7377
Members: 200,000
Publications: *Creative Express; Newsletter; Resource Manual.*

American School Counselor Association (Counseling) (ASCA)
c/o American Counseling Association
5999 Stevensdon Avenue
Alexandria, VA 22304
(703) 823-9800
Members: 13,000
Publications: *ASCA Counselor; Elementary School Guidance and Counseling; The School Counselor.*

American Schools Association (Counseling) (ASA)
3069 Amwiler Road, Suite 4
Atlanta, GA 30360
(404) 449-7141
Nonmembership
Publication: *Directory of College Transfer Information.*

International Association of Counseling Services (IACS)
101 South Whiting Street, Suite 211
Alexandria, VA 22304
(703) 823-9840
Members: 200
Publications: *Counseling Services; Director of Counseling Services.*

National Academic Advising Association (Counseling) (NACADA)
Kansas State University
2323 Anderson Avenue, Suite 226
Manhattan, KS 66502
(913) 532-5717
Members: 3,100
Publications: *NACADA Journal; NACADA Newsletter; National Academic Advising Association—Proceedings of Annual Conference.*

Association for Supervision and Curriculum Development (ASCD)
1250 North Pitt Street
Alexandria, VA 22314-1403
(703) 549-9110

Members: 150,000

Publications: *ASCD Update; Association for Supervision and Curriculum Development—Yearbook; Curriculum Update; Educational Leadership; Journal of Curriculum and Supervision.*

Quest International (Developmental Education)
537 Jones Road
PO Box 566
Granville, OH 43023-0566
(614) 522-6400

Members: 600,000

Publications: *Energizer—A Program Supplement; Skills for Adolescence Curriculum; Skills for Growing Curriculum.*

Association on Higher Education and Disability (Disabled) (AHEAD)
PO Box 21192
Columbus, OH 43221-0192
(614) 488-4972

Members: 1,300

Publications: *ALERT; Journal of Postsecondary Education & Disability; Membership Directory; Proceedings of Annual Conferences on Disabled Students in Postsecondary Education.*

Health Resource Center (Disabled) (HRC)
1 Dupont Circle NW, Suite 800
Washington, DC 20036
(202) 939-9320

Subscribers: 10,000

Publications: *Fact Sheet; Information; Resource Directory.*

American Council on Education (ACE)
1 Dupont Circle NW, Suite 800
Washington, DC 20036
(202) 939-9300

Members: 1,853

Publications: *Educational Record; Higher Education and National Affairs; ACE/Macmillan Series on Higher Education; A Fact Book on Higher Education.*

Association for Direct Instruction (Education) (ADI)
PO Box 10252
Eugene, OR 97440
(503) 485-1293

Members: 2,500

Publication: *Direct Instruction.*

Association for Individually Guided Education (AIGE)
Hutchinson United School District 308
PO Box 1908
Hutchinson, KS 67504
(316) 665-4400

Members: 400

Publications: *Association for Individually Guided Education—Scope; Teacher Talk.*

New England Association of Schools and Colleges (Education) (NEASC)
The Sanborn House
15 High Street
Winchester, MA 01890
(617) 729-6762

Members: 1,600

Publication: *Membership Directory.*

North Central Association of Colleges and Schools (Education) (NCACS)
Arizona State University
Commission on Schools
Tempe, AZ 85287-3011
(602) 965-8700

Members: 8,200

Publication: *NCA Quarterly.*

Northwest Association of Schools and Colleges (Education) (NASC)
Boise State University
Education Building, No. 528
1910 University Drive
Boise, ID 83725
(208) 385-1596

Members: 1,385

Publications: *Directory of Accredited and Affiliated Institutions; Newsletter; Proceedings.*

High School Legal Defense Association (Educational Freedom)
(HSLDA)
PO Box 159
Paeonian Springs, VA 22129
(703) 338-2800

Members: 25,000

Publication: *The Home School Court Report.*

Association of College and University Offices (Educational Funding)
(ACUO)
1001 Connecticut Avenue, Suite 901
Washington, DC 20036
(202) 659-2104

Subscribers: 350

Publication: *News Notes and Deadlines.*

Committee for Education Funding (Educational Funding) (CEF)
505 Capitol Court NE, Suite 200
Washington, DC 20002
(202) 543-6300

Members: 100

Publications: *Budget Impact Alert; Newsletter.*

National Council for Better Education (Educational Reform) (NCBE)
101 North Alfred, Suite 202
Alexandria, VA 22314
(703) 739-2660

Members: 50,000

Publication: *NEA: Propaganda Front of the Radical Left, A Parent's Survival Guide to the Public Schools.*

Junior Engineering Technical Society (JETS)
1420 King Street, Suite 405
Alexandria, VA 22314
(703) 548-5387

Members: 20,000

Publication: *JETS Report: Promoting Interest in Engineering, Technology, Mathematics and Science in High Schools.*

Association of Departments of English (ADE)
10 Astor Place
New York, NY 10003
(212) 614-6317

Members: 840

Publications: *ADE Bulletin; Job Information List.*

College English Association (CEA)
Nazareth College of Rochester
4245 East Avenue
Rochester, NY 14618
(716) 586-2525

Members: 1,500

Publications: *The CEA Critic; The CEA Forum.*

Conference for Secondary School English Department Chairpersons
(CSSEDC)
1180 Brandywyn Lane
Buffalo Grove, IL 60089
(708) 634-0477

Members: 2,000

Publication: *CSSEDC Quarterly.*

National Council of Teachers of English (NCTE)
1111 Kenyon Road
Urbana, IL 61801
(217) 328-3870

Members: 120,000

Publications: *College Composition and Communication; College English; El Quarterly; English Education; English Journal; Language Arts; NOTES Plus; Quarterly Review of Doublespeak; Research in the Teaching of English; SLATE Newsletter: Support for the Learning and Teaching of English; Teaching English in the Two-Year College.*

Teachers of English to Speakers of Other Languages (TESOL)
1600 Cameron Street, Suite 300
Alexandria, VA 22314-2751
(703) 836-0774

Members: 23,000

Publications: *Directory of Professional Preparation; TESOL Journal; TESOL Matters; TESOL Quarterly; Training Program Directory.*

Center for Adult Learning and Education Credentials (Evaluation) (CALEC)
1 Dupont Circle NW
Washington, DC 20036
(202) 939-9475

Members: Unknown

Publications: *Bulletin; Center Newsletter; Directory of Campus-Business Linkages; GED Newsletter; GED Research Briefs; GED Research Studies; PONSI Update.*

Earthwatch (Experiential Education)
680 Mount Auburn Street
Box 403
Watertown, MA 02272
(617) 926-8200

Members: 70,000

Publication: *Earthwatch.*

National Society for Experiential Education (NSEE)
3509 Haworth Drive, Suite 207
Raleigh, NC 27609-7229
(919) 787-3263

Members: 1,300

Publications: *Experiential Education; National Directory of Internships; NSIEE Membership Directory; Strengthening Experiential Education within Your Institution; Combining Service and Learning: A Resource Book for Community and Public Service.*

American Association of Teachers of French (AATF)
57 East Armory Avenue
Champaign, IL 61820
(217) 333-2842

Members: 11,000

Publications: *AATF National Bulletin; Directory; French Review.*

National Council for Geographic Education (NCGE)
Indiana University of Pennsylvania
16A Leonard Hall
Indiana, PA 15705
(412) 357-6290

Members: 3,700

Publications: *Journal of Geography; National Council for Geographic Education—Perspective.*

National Association of Geology Teachers (NAGT)
Department of Geology
Western Washington University
Bellingham, WA 98225
(206) 676-3587

Members: 1,800

Publications: *Journal of Geological Education; Membership Directory.*

American Association of Teachers of German (AATG)
112 Haddontowne Court, No. 104
Cherry Hill, NJ 08034
(609) 795-5553

Members: 7,300

Publications: *American Association of Teachers of German—Newsletter; Die Unterrichtspraxis: For the Teaching of German; German Quarterly.*

Association for Gifted and Talented Students (AGTS)
Northwestern State University
Natchitoches, LA 71497
(318) 357-4572

Members: 2,000

Publication: *Gifted-Talented Digest.*

Professional and Organizational Development Network in Higher Education (POD Network for Post Secondary Education)
15B Exhibit Hall South
Iowa State University
Ames, IA 50011
(515) 294-3808

Members: 700

Publications: *Membership Directory; Newsletter; Improve the Academy; Teaching Excellence; Handbook for New Practitioners; The Muse; Doing Faculty Development.*

American Association of Teachers of Spanish and Portuguese (Hispanic) (AATSP)
PO Box 6349
Mississippi State, MS 39762
(601) 325-2041

Members: 13,000

Publications: *Directory; Hispania.*

Sociedad Honoraria Hispanica (SHH)
Glendale Community College
6000 West Olive Avenue
Glendale, AZ 85302
(602) 435-3727

Members: 1,200

Publication: *Albricias!*

National Council for History Education (NCHE)
26915 Westwood Road, Suite B2
Westlake, OH 44145-4657
(216) 835-1776

Members: 1,500

Publication: *History Matters!*

Technology Student Association (Industrial Education; Elementary, Secondary Schools) (TSA)
1914 Association Drive
Reston, VA 22091
(703) 860-9000

Members: 75,000

Publications: *Advisor Update; School Scene; Chapter Handbook; Student Guide; Technology Teachers Guide; Curricular Resources Guide.*

Vocational Industrial Clubs of America (Industrial Education; Secondary, Postsecondary Schools) (VICA)
PO Box 3000
Leesburg, VA 22075
(703) 777-8810

Members: 272,000

Publications: *VICA Journal; VICA Professional: VP.*

Insurance Education Foundation (High School Teachers and Students)
3601 Vincennes Road
PO Box 68700
Indianapolis, IN 46268-6870
(317) 876-6046

Members: 1,200

Publications: *Governors' Journal; Seminar Manual and Proceedings.*

Teachers Insurance and Annuity Association (TIAA)
730 Third Avenue
New York, NY 10017
(212) 490-9000

Members: 1,500,000

Publication: *TIAA-CREF Annual Report.*

AFS Intercultural Programs (International Exchange) (AFS)
313 East 43rd Street
New York, NY 10017
(212) 949-4242

Members: 100,000

Publications: *AFS Orientation Handbook; AFS Research Reports; AFS World; Directions; Papers in Intercultural Learning.*

American Council for International Studies (International Exchange) (ACIS)
19 Bay State Road
Boston, MA 02215
(617) 236-2051

Members: 20,000

Publication: *Passport.*

Modern Language Association of America (MLA)
10 Astor Place, Fifth Floor
New York, NY 10003
(212) 475-9500

Members: 30,000

Publications: *Convention Program; Directory; MLA International Bibliography; MLA Job Information List; MLA Newsletter; Modern Language Association of America—Profession; PMLA Publications of the Modern Language Association of America.*

Laubach Literacy Action (LLA)
Box 131
1320 Jamesville Avenue
Syracuse, NY 13210
(315) 422-9121

Members: 55,000

Publications: *Directory; The Forum: Management Issues for Adult Literacy Programs; Literacy Advance; New Readers Speaking Out; Trainer Touchstone.*

Laubach Literacy International (LLI)
Box 131
1320 Jamesville Avenue
Syracuse, NY 13210
(315) 422-9121

Members: 80,000

Publications: *Laubach Literacy Action Directory; Laubach Literacy International—Annual Report; Literacy Advance; Literacy Advocate; New Readers Press—Catalog; News for You.*

Literacy Volunteers of America (LVA)
5795 Widewaters Parkway
Syracuse, NY 13214
(315) 445-8000

Members: 100,000

Publications: *Directory; The Reader.*

Distributive Education Clubs of America (Marketing) (DECA) High School, Junior Collegiate; Professional
1908 Association Drive
Reston, VA 22091
(703) 860-5000

Members: 180,000

Publications: *DECA Advisor; DECA Guide; New Dimensions.*

American Mathematical Association of Two Year Colleges (Mathematics) (AMATYC)
Mott Community College
1401 East Court Street
Flint, MI 48503
(313) 232-3980

Members: 2,800

Publications: *AMATYC News; AMATYC Review.*

National Council of Supervisors of Mathematics (NCSM)
PO Box 10667
Golden, CO 80401
(414) 229-4844

Members: 2,000

Publications: *Membership Directory; Newsletter.*

National Council of Teachers of Mathematics (NCTM)
1906 Association Drive
Reston, VA 22091-1593
(703) 620-9840

Members: 98,000

Publications: *Arithmetic Teacher; Journal for Research in Mathematics Education; Mathematics Teacher; National Council of Teachers of Mathematics—Yearbook; NCTM News Bulletin.*

Health Occupations Students of America (Medical Education) (HOSA) (Secondary and Postsecondary)
6309 North O'Connor Road, Suite 215, LB-117
Irving, TX 75039-3510
(214) 506-9780

Members: 40,000

Publications: *HOSA Leaders Directory; HOSA Leaders' Update; HOSA News Magazine.*

National Middle School Association (Middle Schools) (NMSA)
4807 Evanswood Drive
Columbus, OH 43229
(614) 848-8211

Members: 10,000

Publications: *Middle Ground; Middle School Journal; Target.*

American Montessori Society (AMS)
150 Fifth Avenue, Suite 203
New York, NY 10011
(212) 924-3209

Members: 12,000

Publications: *Montessori Life; School Directory; Teacher Training Directory.*

Association Montessori International-U.S.A. (AMI-USA)
170 West Scholfield Road
Rochester, NY 14617
(716) 544-6709

Members: 1,500

Publications: *AMI International Study Conference Proceedings; AMI/USA Directory of Member Schools.*

International Association of Jazz Educators (Music, Grade School through College) (IAJE)
Box 724
Manhattan, KS 66502
(913) 776-8744

Members: 6,800

Publication: *Jazz Educators Journal.*

Music Teachers National Association (MTNA)
617 Vine Street, Suite 1432
Cincinnati, OH 45202
(513) 421-1420

Members: 25,000

Publications: *American Music Teacher Magazine; Foundation; National Certification Newsletter; Music Teachers National Association—Directory of Nationally Certified Teachers.*

National Association of College Wind and Percussion Instructors (Music) (NACWPI)
Northeast Missouri State University
Division of Fine Arts
Kirksville, MO 63501
(816) 785-4442

Members: 1,200

Publications: *Faculty Recital Booklet; Journal; Research Library Catalog.*

National Association of Schools of Music (NASM)
11250 Roger Bacon Drive, No. 21
Reston, VA 22090
(703) 437-0700

Members: 550

Publications: *National Association of Schools of Music—Directory; National Association of Schools of Music—Handbook; National Association of Schools of Music—Proceedings.*

National Band and Choral Directors Hall of Fame
519 North Halifax Avenue
Daytona Beach, FL 32118
(904) 252-0381

NonMembership

Publications: *National Band and Choral Directors Hall of Fame Directory; National Music Newsletter.*

National PTA—National Congress of Parents and Teachers
700 North Rush Street
Chicago, IL 60611
(312) 787-0977

Members: 7,000,000

Publications: *National PTA Directory; PTA Today; PTA Handbook; Looking in on Your School: A Workbook for Improving Public Education.*

American Association of School Personnel Administrators (AASPA)
2330 Alhambra Boulevard
Sacramento, CA 95817
(916) 736-2000

Members: 1,700

Publications: *AASPA Bulletin; American Association of School Personnel Administrators—Bulletin and Newsletter; American Association of School Personnel Administrators—Membership Roster; AASPA Newsletter; AASPA Report; Directory of Personnel Practices and Programs; Research Brief; Standards for School Personnel Administration; Comprehensive Report on Minority Recruitment.*

American College Personnel Association
1 Dupont Circle NW, Suite 360-A
Washington, DC 20036-1110

Members: 7,000

Publications: *ACPA Developments; Journal of College Student Development.*

American Association of Philosophy Teachers (AAPT)
University of Oklahoma
Library 418
PO Box 26901
Oklahoma City, OK 73190
(405) 271-2111

Members: 300

Publication: *AAPT News.*

Society for Photographic Education (Photography, Secondary and College Level) (SPE)
PO Box 222116
Dallas, TX 75222-2116
(214) 943-8442

Members: 1,600

Publications: *Exposure; Membership Directory; Newsletter.*

American Alliance for Health, Physical Education, Recreation and Dance (AAHPERD)
1900 Association Drive
Reston, VA 22091
(703) 476-3400

Members: 42,000

Publications: *AAHPERD Update; Health Education; Journal of Physical Education Recreation and Dance; Leisure Today; News Kit on Programs for the Aging; Research Quarterly; Strategies.*

National Association for Sport and Physical Education (NASPE)
1900 Association Drive
Reston, VA 22091
(703) 476-3410

Members: 30,000

Publications: *The Athletic Director; Strategies; NASPE News; Strategies: A Journal for Physical and Sport Educators; Update.*

National Council of Secondary School Athletic Directors (Physical Education) (NCSSAD)
1900 Association Drive
Reston, VA 22091
(703) 476-3410

Members: 1,500

Publication: *Athletic Director Newsletter.*

National Interscholastic Athletic Administrators Association (Physical Education) (NIAAA)
Box 20626
11724 Northwest Plaza Circle
Kansas City, MO 64195-0626
(816) 464-5400

Members: 5,000

Publications: *Interscholastic Athletic Administration; National Conference Proceedings; Speakers' Directory; State Athletic Director Association.*

American Association of Physics Teachers (AAPT)
5112 Berwyn Road
College Park, MD 20740
(301) 345-4200

Members: 11,000

Publication: *Announcer.*

National Head Start Association (Preschool Education) (NHSA)
201 North Union Street, Suite 320
Alexandria, VA 22314
(703) 739-0875
Members: 8,000
Publications: *NHSA Newsletter; Tell the Head Start Story.*

Columbia Scholastic Press Advisors Association (CSPAA)
Columbia University
Box 11, Central Mail Room
New York, NY 10027-6969
(212) 280-3311
Members: 2,800
Publication: *Springboard to Journalism.*

Columbia Scholastic Press Association (CSPA)
Columbia University
Box 11, Central Mail Room
New York, NY 10027-6969
(212) 280-3311
Members: 2,800
Publications: *Student Press Review; The Advisor's Companion, Official CSPA Stylebook.*

National Scholastic Press Association (NSPA)
620 Rarig Center
330 21st Avenue South
University of Minnesota
Minneapolis, MN 55455
(612) 625-8335
Members: 3,600
Publication: *Trends in High School Media.*

Country Day School Headmasters Association of the United States (Principals) (CDSHA)
Charlotte Country Day School
1440 Carmel Road
Charlotte, NC 28226
(704) 366-1241
Members: 100
Publications: Unknown

Headmasters Association (Principals) (HA)
National Cathedral School
Mount St. Alban NW
Washington, DC 20016
(202) 537-6334

Members: 263

Publications: *Membership List; Headmasters Association Grey Book.*

National Association of Elementary School Principals (NAESP)
1615 Duke Street
Alexandria, VA 22314
(703) 684-3345

Members: 26,000

Publications: *Communicator; Focus on Finance; Here's How; Principal; Report to Parents; Research Roundup; Streamlined Seminar.*

National Association of Principals of Schools for Girls (NAPSG)
4050 Little River Road
Hendersonville, NC 28739
(704) 693-1490

Members: 600

Publication: *Proceedings.*

National Association of Secondary School Principals (NASSP)
1904 Association Drive
Reston, VA 22091
(703) 860-0200

Members: 43,000

Publications: *Administrative Information Report; AP Special; Leadership for Student Activities; NASSP Bulletin: The Journal for Middle Level and High School Administrators; NASSP—Curriculum Report; NASSP—Legal Memorandum; NASSP—Newsleader; The Practioner; Schools in the Middle; Tips for Principals.*

Association of Boarding Schools (Private Schools)
c/o NAIS
75 Federal Street, Fifth Floor
Boston, MA 02110
(617) 451-2444

Members: 241

Publication: *Boarding Schools Directory.*

Council for American Private Education (Private Schools) (CAPE)
1726 M Street NW, No. 1102
Washington, DC 20036
(202) 659-0016

Members: 14

Publications: *Outlook; Private Schools of the United States.*

College Reading and Learning Association (CRLA)
Chemeketa Community College
PO Box 14007
Salem, OR 97309
(503) 399-2556

Members: 1,000

Publications: *CRLA Newsletter; Journal of College Reading and Learning.*

International Reading Association (IRA)
800 Barksdale Road
Newark, DE 19714-8139
(302) 731-1600

Members: 93,000

Publications: *Desktop Reference to the International Reading Association; Journal of Reading; Lecturay Vida; Reading Research Quarterly; Reading Teacher; Reading Today.*

Reading Is Fundamental (RIF)
600 Maryland Avenue SW, Suite 500
Washington, DC 20024
(202) 287-3220

Members: 3,559

Publication: *RIF Newsletter.*

National Association of State Supervisors and Directors of Secondary Education (NASSDSE)
School Accreditation Department
Richard F. Kniep Building
700 Governor's Drive
Pierre, SD 57501
(605) 773-4709

Members: 75

Publications: Unknown.

Access Research Network (Science) (ARN)
PO Box 38069
Colorado Springs, CO 80937
(719) 633-1772
Members: 300
Publications: *Annual Report; Origins Research.*

Association for the Education of Teachers in Science (AETS)
5040 Haley Center
Auburn University
Auburn, AL 36849
(205) 844-6799
Members: 677
Publications: *Association for the Education of Teachers in Science—Newsletter; Association for the Education of Teachers in Science—Yearbook; Journal of Science Teacher Education; Pocket Guide to AETS; Science Education.*

Council for Elementary Science International (CESI)
11 Marion Road
Westport, CT 06880
(203) 226-4938
Members: 1,600
Publications: *CESI Directory; CESI News; CESI Source Books; CESI Updates; Monograph.*

Federation for Unified Science Education (FUSE)
Capital University
231 Battelle Hall of Science
Columbus, OH 43209
(614) 236-6816
Members: 450
Publications: *Prism II; Proceedings of Annual Conference.*

National Earth Science Teachers Association (NESTA)
340 Prairiewood Circle
Fargo, ND 58103
(701) 241-9818
Members: 1,500
Publication: *The Earth Scientist.*

National Science Teachers Association (NSTA)
1742 Connecticut Avenue NW
Washington, DC 20009-1171
(202) 328-5800

Members: 63,000

Publications: *Energy and Education Newsletter; Journal of College Science Teaching; NSTA Report; Science and Children; Science Scope; The Science Teacher.*

School Science and Mathematics Association (SSMA)
Bowling Green State University
126 Life Science Building
Bowling Green, OH 43403
(419) 372-7393

Members: 1,100

Publications: *School Science and Mathematics; School Science and Mathematics Association—Convention Program; SSMArrt Newsletter.*

Tripoli Rocketry Association (TRA) (Science)
PO Box 339
Kenner, LA 70065-0339
(504) 467-1967

Members: 1,892

Publications: *Tripoli Newsletter; The Tripolitan.*

National Council for the Social Studies (NCSS)
3501 Newark Street NW
Washington, DC 20016
(202) 966-7840

Members: 26,000

Publications: *Bulletin; Social Education; The Social Studies Professional; Social Studies and the Young Learner; Theory and Research in Social Education.*

American Council on Rural Special Education (ACRES)
Western Washington University
National Rural Development Institute
Miller Hall 359
Bellingham, WA 98225
(801) 650-5659

Members: 1,000

Publications: *ACRES Membership Newsletter; Rural Special Education Quarterly; RuraLink.*

AVKO Educational Research Foundation (Special Education) (AVKOEFR)
3084 West Willard Road
Birch Run, MI 48415
(313) 686-9283

Members: 500

Publications: *AVKO Educational Research Foundation—Newsletter; Basic Patterns of English Spelling; Dictionary of Phonograms; Sequential Spelling.*

Council of Administrators of Special Education (CASE)
615 16th Street NW
Albuquerque, NM 87104
(505) 243-7622

Members: 4,700

Publications: *CASE Newsletter; CASE in Point.*

Council for Children with Behavioral Disorders (Special Education) (CCBD)
c/o Council for Exceptional Children
1920 Association Drive
Reston, VA 22091-1589
(703) 620-3660

Members: 8,500

Publications: *Behavioral Disorders; CBBD Newsletter; Monographs.*

Council for Exceptional Children (Special Education) (CEC)
1920 Association Drive
Reston, VA 22091-1589
(703) 620-3660

Members: 54,000

Publications: *Exceptional Child Education Resources; Exceptional Children; Teaching Exceptional Children.*

National Forensic League (Speech) (NFL)
PO Box 38
Ripon, WI 54971
(414) 748-6206

Members: 798,000

Publications: *NFL Journal; Rostrum.*

Speech Communication Association (SCA)
5105 Backlick Road, Building E
Annandale, VA 22003
(703) 750-0533

Members: Unknown

Publications: *Communication Education; Communication Monographs; Critical Studies in Mass Communication; Free Speech Yearbook; Journal of Applied Communication Research; Quarterly Journal of Speech; Spectra; Speech Communication Directory; Speech Communication Teacher; Text and Performance Quarterly.*

American School Food Service Association (Student Services) (ASFSA)
1600 Duke Street, Seventh Floor
Alexandria, VA 22314
(800) 877-8822

Members: 65,000

Publications: *School Food Service Journal; School Food Service Research Review.*

Association of Teacher Educators (Teachers) (ATE)
1900 Association Drive, Suite ATE
Reston, VA 22091
(703) 620-3110

Members: 4,000

Publications: *Action in Teacher Education; ATE News Letter.*

International Council on Education for Teaching (Teachers) (ICET)
2009 North 14th Street, Suite 609
Arlington, VA 22201
(703) 525-5253

Members: Unknown

Publications: *International Yearbook on Teacher Education; Newsletter; Proceedings; W. Clement Stone Lecture.*

Secondary School Admission Test Board (Testing) (SSATB)
12 Stockton Street
Princeton, NJ 08540
(609) 683-4440

Members: 650

Publications: *Bulletin of Information; Memberanda Newsletter; SSATB Annual Report; SSATB Network Directory; User's Guide; Preparing for the SSAT; SSAT Policy Guide.*

International Thespian Society (Theatre) (ITS)
3368 Central Parkway
Cincinnati, OH 45225-2392
(513) 559-1996

Members: 28,000

Publications: *Dramatics Magazine; Super Trouper.*

American Board of Vocational Experts (Vocational Education) (ABVE)
3500 Southwest Sixth Street, Suite 100
Topeka, KS 66606-2806
(913) 232-9937

Members: 380

Publications: *National Directory of Vocational Experts; The Vocational Expert.*

American Vocational Association (Vocational Education) (AVA)
1410 King Street
Alexandria, VA 22314
(703) 683-3111

Members: 46,000

Publications: *American Vocational Association—Update: The Newspaper for Vocational Educators; Job Market Update; Newsletter; Vocational Education Journal.*

Business Professionals of America (Vocational Education) (BPA)
5454 Cleveland Avenue
Columbus, OH 43231
(614) 895-7277

Members: 54,000

Publications: *Advisor's Bulletin; Competitive Events Guidelines; Communique; It's a New Year; Monthly Memo; Student Magazine.*

10

Resume Samples for Teachers, Administrators, Career Counselors, and Media Specialists

The following pages in this chapter include many of the resume samples from the client files of Just Resumes®. Other samples were prepared specifically for this book. All these resumes offer accurate job descriptions and educational requirement information. Be aware, however, that the educational requirements vary from state to state and the job titles and descriptions may vary among school districts.

The samples include resumes for professionals from elementary, secondary, and postsecondary schools and colleges; each resume focuses on particular individual goals. There are a variety of formats to choose from in functional, chronological, and combination styles. An index to the resume samples is in the back of the book. The resume samples are conveniently categorized and alphabetized by job title.

Look at each resume carefully. Again, think about how your own background applies to the job or internship you'd like to obtain.

Remember, to take full advantage of the valuable information in this book and gain the overall perspective you'll need to write your own effective resume, it's important that you've already read all the text in Chapters 1 and 2 before reviewing the resume samples in this chapter.

BLAIR STEPHEN THEODORE
112 Vis Presideo
Goleta, CA 93110
(805) 987-2223

OBJECTIVE
Administrator, English Teacher

EDUCATION
Multiple Subject Teaching Credential, 1984
University of California, Santa Barbara, CA

BA, English, 1984
Tulane University, New Orleans, LA

PROFESSIONAL EXPERIENCE

DEAN OF STUDENTS   1989-present
Bishop Garcia Diego High School, Santa Barbara, CA
- Supervise students and faculty in all school activities.
- Implement and enforce attendance and behavior rules and regulations for school and extracurricular social events for as many as 300 students.
- Serve as troubleshooting source for faculty and liaison between parents and faculty members.

ENGLISH TEACHER   1987-89
- Taught English to classes of 18-45 students and one-on-one instruction.
- Served as Chairman for the English Department.
- Functioned as advisor for the school yearbook and newspaper.

ENGLISH TEACHER   1984-87
Santa Clara High School, Oxnard, CA
- Taught classes of 18-40 students, Grades 11-12.
- Assisted students with individualized instruction.
- Served as advisor for the school yearbook, assistant Varsity Coach, and Junior Football Coach.

AFFILIATIONS
Social Chairman, Rotary Club
Member, American Teachers Association
Member, The South Coast Writing Project (SCWrip)
Member, The National Council of Teachers of English (NCTE)

- More -

PROFESSIONAL PROFILE

- Highly organized and dedicated with the ability to effectively teach students of a wide range of achievement levels and ethnic backgrounds.
- Excellent written, oral, and interpersonal communication skills with cross cultural sensitivity.
- 9+ years experience teaching English to high school students, specializing in Writing and Editing, American Literature, Modern American Literature, Critical Thinking Skills, Vocabulary Building, and The Composing Process.

LOCATION OF PLACEMENT PAPERS

Educational Careers
Counseling and Career Services
University of California at Santa Barbara
Santa Barbara, CA 93106
(805) 961-4416

MERRI ELLEN STANFORD
2190 Vine Street
Ft. Collins, CO 80521
(303) 224-2213

OBJECTIVE
Agri-Science Instructor

EDUCATION
Colorado Vocational Teaching Credential, 1979
University of Northern Colorado, Greeley, CO

BS Agriculture, 1974
Colorado State University, Ft. Collins, CO

PROFESSIONAL EXPERIENCE
AGRI-SCIENCE INSTRUCTOR   1984-present
Aims Community College, Greeley, CO
- Teach daily classes to high school students in the Agri-Science Program, emphasizing Animal Science, Plant Science, and Environmental Science, plus an overview of the Agri-Science industry.
- Participate in FFA and cooperative education.
- Contribute to department, campus, and college activities and initiatives.
  - Develop course curriculums and advise faculty and staff on issues involving Agri-Science.
  - Select textbooks for courses offered.
  - Serve on committees that provide leadership to part-time faculty.

PROFESSIONAL PROFILE
- Provide excellent academic background and knowledge in Animal Science, Plant Science, and Environmental Science.
- Hands-on experience with vocational education co-op and FFA.
- Demonstrate good classroom management skills with experience in a wide range of teaching techniques with appropriate assessment skills.

COMMUNITY SERVICE
Member, Agri-Science Association of Colorado, 1979
Member, Colorado Forestry Service Association, 1979

PREVIOUS EMPLOYMENT HISTORY
Agri-Science Instructor, Front Range Community College, Boulder, CO   1979-84

ROBIN S. BENSON
217 Whitcomb Avenue
Ft. Collins, CO 80524
(303) 224-3213

OBJECTIVE
Aquaculture Instructor

EDUCATION
Colorado Vocational Teaching Credential, 1979

MS, Aquaculture Science, 1979
Colorado State University, Ft. Collins, CO

BS, Aquaculture Science, 1974
Colorado State University, Ft. Collins, CO

PROFESSIONAL EXPERIENCE
AQUACULTURE INSTRUCTOR   1984-present
Front Range Community College, Ft. Collins, CO
- Teach daily courses in Aquaculture.
- Coordinate outside activities with the aquaculture industry.
- Direct, maintain, and manage the indoor, intensive recirculating aquaculture system in the aquaculture lab.
- Develop course curriculum and advise faculty and staff in the Aquaculture Department.
- Select textbooks for courses offered.
- Serve on committees and provide continued leadership to part-time faculty.

AFFILIATION
Member, Aquaculture Association of Colorado, 1979

PREVIOUS EMPLOYMENT HISTORY
Aquaculture Instructor, Aims Community College, Greeley, CO   1979-84
Aquaculture Intern, Denver Community College, Denver, CO   1974-79

CARMEN R. SANCHEZ

1903 Pedregosa Avenue
Santa Barbara, CA 93105
(805) 682-7594

OBJECTIVE
Elementary-School Teacher

EDUCATION
BA, Art and Elementary Education
Grand Canyon College, Phoenix, AZ, 1979

California Multiple Subject Teaching Credential (K-12)
University of California, Santa Barbara, CA, 1979

TEACHING EXPERIENCE

ART TEACHER (Grade K-8)   1979-84
Bartlett Private Elementary School, Phoenix, AZ
- Established an art program and taught techniques and elements of design.
- Developed and implemented activities based on respect and enjoyment of the student's creativity, allowing originality through experimentation and manipulation of materials.
- Planned a variety of projects with a balance between two- and three-dimensional work, using traditional and unique materials.
- Provided classroom experiences, such as nonverbal instruction, nonverbal student interaction, and group activities.
- Emphasized problem solving and conceptual approaches.
- Introduced students to the history of art through films, slides, photographs, and guest speakers.
- Organized field trips to art museums, galleries, and studios.
- Participated in the production of children's musicals and plays.
   - Facilitated initial brainstorming sessions.
   - Designed and constructed sets, props, and costumes.
   - Worked with lighting and special effects; choreographed dance pieces.

TEACHER'S AIDE (Grades 1-2)   1972-74
Greenville Elementary School, Greenville, IL
- Developed ability to work with children, peers, and parents.
- Demonstrated organizational skills and commitment to subjects taught.

- More -

PROFESSIONAL PROFILE
- Team player with teachers, administrators, and parents.
- Highly organized, dedicated with a positive attitude.
- Communicate effectively with all types of people.
- Work well in a competitive and challenging environment.
- Strength in assessing people's needs while gaining trust and confidence.
- Skilled problem solver with proven leadership qualities.

AFFILIATIONS
Member, American Teachers Association

LOCATION OF PLACEMENT PAPERS
Educational Careers
Counseling and Career Services
Grand Canyon College
Phoenix, AZ 85021
(602) 870-5543

LAWRENCE C. PAUL
3214 LaPorte Avenue
Ft. Collins, CO 80521
(303) 224-2139

OBJECTIVE
Arts and Humanities Instructor

EDUCATION
MA, Philosophy/French, 1979
University of Northern Colorado, Greeley, CO

BA, Art History, 1974
University of Denver, Denver, CO

PROFESSIONAL EXPERIENCE

ARTS AND HUMANITIES INSTRUCTOR   1979-present
Front Range Community College, Ft. Collins, CO
- Teach Arts and Humanities courses on a daily basis.

- Develop new Arts and Humanities courses and curriculum content.

- Actively participate in division and college activities and committees.

- Serve as faculty chair for Arts and Humanities.

- Develop/monitor budget, course schedules, faculty teaching, and assignments.

- Select and order textbooks; update catalog and provide leadership to the department.

AFFILIATIONS
Member, National Education Association
Member, Poudre Education Association
Member, Colorado Teachers of Arts and Humanities Association

PREVIOUS EMPLOYMENT HISTORY
French Instructor, Aims Community College, Greeley, CO   1976-79
Philosophy Instructor, University of Denver, Denver, CO   1974-76

MEGAN ANNE CARRIE
256 Terry Shores Road
Ft. Collins, CO 80524
(303) 224-3032

OBJECTIVE
High School Assistant Principal

EDUCATION
MEA, Education Administration, 1974
University of Northern Colorado, Greeley, CO

BA, Sociology, 1970
University of Northern Colorado, Greeley, CO

CERTIFICATION
Colorado Secondary, Elementary Education, 1974

PROFESSIONAL EXPERIENCE
ASSISTANT PRINCIPAL   1982-present
Ft. Collins High School, Ft. Collins, CO
- Administer student personnel program, and counsel and discipline students.
- Plan and supervise school student activity programs.
- Give individual and group guidance for personal problems, educational and vocational objectives, and social and recreational activities.
- Talk with and discipline students in cases of attendance and behavior problems.
- Supervise students in attendance at assemblies and athletic events.
- Monitor safety and security; direct and coordinate teacher supervision of halls and cafeteria.
- Observe and evaluate teacher performance.
- Maintain records of student attendance.
- Arrange for and oversee substitute teachers.
- Work with administrators to coordinate and supervise student teachers program; organize and administer in-service teacher training.
- Act as Principal in absence of Principal.

COMMUNITY RELATIONS
Assistant Director, Rotary Club, Ft. Collins, CO, since 1974

PREVIOUS EMPLOYMENT HISTORY
Assistant Principal, Rocky Mountain High School, Ft. Collins, CO   1978-82
Assistant Principal, Lincoln Junior High School, Ft. Collins, CO   1974-78

WALTER A. BRUCE
3298 McConnel Drive
Ft. Collins, CO 80521
(303) 224-2195

OBJECTIVE
Assistant to the President

EDUCATION
MA, Education Administration, 1979
University of Northern Colorado, Greeley, CO

BA, Education Administration, 1974
University of Denver, Denver, CO

PROFESSIONAL EXPERIENCE

ASSISTANT TO THE PRESIDENT   1979-present
Front Range Community College, Ft. Collins, CO
- Assist the College President with directing, planning, coordinating, supervising, and evaluating general planning and special projects.

- Responsible for strategic planning, environmental scanning, marketing, community and college relations, resource development, policy and procedures oversight, governmental relations, foundation development, and research.

- Serve as aid with college-wide projects.

PROFESSIONAL PROFILE
- Effective oral and written communication skills.
- Ability to work with diverse constituencies and maintain a positive attitude.
- Excellent management skills, demonstrating professionalism, diplomacy, and tact.

PREVIOUS EMPLOYMENT HISTORY
Personnel Administrator, Aims Community College, Greeley, CO   1974-79

WALTER E. MURRY
97009 Resort Road
Portland, OR 97201
(503) 760-3333

Objective: Athletics Department Director

PROFESSIONAL ACTIVITIES
Faculty Supervisor, PCC Quad Rugby Program
Active Member, PCC Student Athletic Assistance Program
Committee Member, PCC Employee Wellness Program
Academic Advisor, Portland City College (PCC)

CURRENT EMPLOYMENT
PORTLAND CITY COLLEGE, Portland, OR   1983-present
Founder/Director
- Established and supervise the Health Appraisal and Exercise Sciences Lab program at Portland City College.
- Program includes health promotion, fitness testing, and development of a comprehensive health and fitness program for students and articulation with area high schools and colleges.

Student Health Services Coordinator
- Promote student health and fitness.
- Established a highly successful college-wide fitness testing program.
- Supervise the wellness program for college faculty and staff.
- Active participant in the Student Athlete Assistance Program.

Instructor
- Teach college students Health, Adapted Physical Education, Senior Fitness, Exercise Sciences, and Physical Education Activities.

EDUCATION
MS Degree, Physical Education, 1982
Cal Poly State University, San Luis Obispo, CA

California Teaching Credential, 1972
University of California, Santa Barbara, CA
Minor: Athletic Coaching

BA Degree, Business Economics 1970
University of California, Santa Barbara, CA

CREDENTIALS/CERTIFICATIONS
- Adapted Physical Education Credential, 1989
  Cal Poly State University San Luis Obispo, CA
- California Community College Supervisor Credential, 1989
- Exercise Test Technologist Certification, 1986
  American College of Sportsmedicine
- Adapted Aquatics Credential, 1984
- California Community College Teaching Credential, 1983
  Emphasis: Special Education
- California Teaching Credential (Life), Secondary Level, 1972

PROFESSIONAL ORGANIZATIONS
- Member, American College of Sportsmedicine
- Member, California Association for Health, Physical
  Education, Recreation & Dance
- Member, California Association of Post-Secondary
  Educators of the Disabled

PROFESSIONAL PAPERS
- Electromyographic Study of Abdominal Exercises.
- The Cardiovascular Fitness Value of Jazzercise Using Telemetry.
- Biomechanical Analysis of Bat and Ball Velocities in Baseball.
- The Effect of Locomotor Activities on Strength Gains of Adolescent Boys.
- Comparative Measurement of Body Composition During Pregnancy Using
  Bioelectrical Impedance, Skinfold Measurements & Hydrostatic Weighing.

PREVIOUS EMPLOYMENT
Post-Graduate Internship, UC San Diego Rehab. Program   Spring-1982
Phys. Ed. Coach, Santa Barbara High School District   1973-81

JUNE ANNE HOLST

2214 Peterson Street
Ft. Collins, CO 80524
(303) 224-2226

OBJECTIVE
Career Counselor

EDUCATION
PhD, Career Counseling, 1974
Colorado State University, Ft. Collins, CO

MA, Counseling Psychology, 1970
Colorado State University, Ft. Collins, CO

Colorado Secondary Teaching Credential, Counseling, 1970

PROFESSIONAL EXPERIENCE

CAREER COUNSELOR   1978-present
Rocky Mountain High School, Ft. Collins, CO

- Conduct planned, effective, and goal-oriented counseling sessions to individuals and small groups of students.
- Provide opportunities and experience for students to develop self-understanding regarding interests, abilities, and aptitudes for future planning.
- Involve students in personalized educational and career planning.
- Assist in planning, developing, implementing, and evaluating programs and services to meet the developmental needs of students.
- Select, develop, and implement topics consistent with identified high priority students needs and district goals.
- Assist in transitions between elementary/junior high, junior high/senior high and senior high/postgraduation.
- Conduct parent/teacher conferences; function as a resource to parent/teacher groups in the school community.
- Consult and confer with administration and support personnel regarding student needs and concerns.
- Coordinate and support the district and building testing program.
- Enhance positive self-concept and attitude toward learning among students.
- Participate in staff development activities, educational courses, and professional organizations.
- Maintain student counseling records.

- More -

PROFESSIONAL PROFILE
- Work cooperatively with colleagues, parents and community.
- Portray a positive attitude in the school environment.
- Treat individuals with respect and dignity.
- Provide conditions under which students can exercise self-discipline, honesty, leadership, and citizenship.
- Demonstrate a concern for student health and safety.
- Provide opportunities for the student to assume responsibility and develop independence.

AFFILIATIONS
Member, American Librarian Association

PREVIOUS EMPLOYMENT HISTORY
Career Counselor, Ft. Collins High School, Ft. Collins, CO   1974-78
Career Counselor, Lesher Junior High School, Ft. Collins, CO   1970-74

GERALD STUART WALTON
110 Peterson Street
Ft. Collins, CO 80524
(303) 224-9226

OBJECTIVE
Career Counselor

EDUCATION
PhD Career Counseling, 1974
Colorado State University, Ft. Collins, CO

MA, Counseling Psychology, 1970
Colorado State University, Ft. Collins, CO

Colorado Secondary Teaching Credential, Counseling, 1970

PROFESSIONAL EXPERIENCE

CAREER COUNSELOR   1978-present
Lincoln Junior High School, Ft. Collins, CO
- Select and use counseling appropriate to students' problems and circumstances.
- Use effective group and individual techniques.
- Provide information that relates educational opportunities and achievements to the world of work.
- Share pertinent information on student behavior, student issues, school policies, and student orientation.
- Facilitate problem-solving and conflict resolution with parents and teachers
- Maintain timely follow-up on decisions made regarding students.
- Make appropriate referrals to community resources.
- Assist students and parents with educational planning.
- Assist in the dissemination and collection of test materials; ensure standardization of district testing program.
- Coordinate and support the orientation and registration of students.
- Participate in staff development activities, educational courses, and professional organizations.
- Collaborate with others to fulfill responsibilities related to building and district goals and priorities.
- Use self-evaluation to improve counseling and constructive advice for improvement; develop an annual growth plan.

- More -

PROFESSIONAL PROFILE

- Demonstrate ability to establish and maintain effective, cooperative relationships with school personnel, students, and parents.
- Possess excellent written and oral communication skills.
- Demonstrate understanding and empathy necessary for working with students.
- Establish a caring and secure environment for students.
- Convey enjoyment and enthusiasm for teaching and learning.

AFFILIATION

Member, North Central Association for Career Counselors

PREVIOUS EMPLOYMENT HISTORY

Career Counselor, Ft. Collins High School, Ft. Collins, CO   1974-78
Teacher, Rocky Mountain High School, Ft. Collins, CO   1970-74

SHEILA S. LAWRY
4432 Front Street
Ft. Collins, CO 80521
(303) 224-2139

OBJECTIVE
Chemistry Instructor/Department Chair

EDUCATION
MA, Science/Chemistry, 1979
University of Northern Colorado, Greeley, CO

BA, Chemistry, 1974
University of Denver, Denver, CO

PROFESSIONAL EXPERIENCE

CHEMISTRY INSTRUCTOR/DEPARTMENT CHAIR   1979-present
Front Range Community College, Ft. Collins, CO
- Teach daily courses in Chemistry, develop new course material in the Chemistry area and new curriculum content.

- Actively participate in division and college activities and committees.

- Serve as the faculty chair for the science department at the Larimer Campus.

- Develop and monitor budget, course schedules, and faculty teaching assignments.

- Select and order textbooks, materials, and supplies for classes and labs.

- Evaluate adjunct faculty, supervise lab technicians, and update catalog.

- Coordinate lab safety policies and procedures in conjunction with the college safety committees.

- Provide leadership to the department.

PREVIOUS EMPLOYMENT HISTORY
Chemistry Instructor, Aims Community College, Greeley, CO   1974-79

CLAUDIA DIANE SOPHIA
702 Dry Lake Avenue
Santa Barbara, CA 93110
(805) 569-0004

Objective: Computer Instructor

EDUCATION/CREDENTIALS

BA, Psychology, 1971
University of California, Santa Barbara, CA

Community College Instructor Credential, 1989

Lifetime Limited Service Credential
Architectural Engineering Related Technologies

PROFESSIONAL EXPERIENCE

Computer Instructor
- Teach Computer Assisted Drafting and Design (CADD).
  - Instruct classes of 24 students in computer lab with 12 stations twice a week.
  - Deal effectively with multicultural and handicapped students.
  - Currently teach intermediate and advanced AutoCAD systems and will be teaching beginning AutoCAD, summer of 1995.
- Taught CADVance and PCAD software programs to college-level students as well as the following college-level drafting courses: Blueprint Reading... Freehand Drafting...Mechanical Drafting...Electronic Drafting.

Computer Drafting and Consulting
- Develop conceptual design of mechanical and architectural projects.
- Produced existing layout from blueprints to AutoCAD.
- Set up customized versions of the AutoCAD system for various companies throughout Northern and Southern California.
  - Developed an effective employee training manual.
  - Provide training seminars and workshops for company employees.

EMPLOYMENT HISTORY

Home Management, Family, Study, Travel	1980-present
Computer Instructor, <u>Santa Barbara City College</u>, Technologies Div.	1975-80
Teacher's Aide, <u>Santa Barbara Elementary School District</u>	1970-75

RALPH PAUL JOHNS, CPA
1250 Lake Street
Ft. Collins, CO 80521
(303) 224-2198

OBJECTIVE
Controller

EDUCATION
MA, Accounting, 1979
University of Northern Colorado, Greeley, CO

BA, Business Economics, 1974
University of Denver, Denver, CO

PROFESSIONAL EXPERIENCE

CONTROLLER   1979-present
Front Range Community College, Westminster, CO

- Direct accounting activities for accounts payable, student accounts, cashiering, payroll, and the accounting staff.

- Maintain accounting and financial reports for three campuses, including general restricted, agency, and auxiliary funds.

- Interpret, implement, and reinforce the State of Colorado fiscal rules.

- Ensure higher education accounting standards are followed.

- Advise the Vice President of administration on all accounting issues; serve as liaison between the community college and the State Controller's Office and the CCCOE System's Controller.

PROFESSIONAL PROFILE
- Maintain excellent interpersonal and oral/written communication skills.
- Gained thorough knowledge of the State of Colorado accounting systems and Information Associates financial system.

AFFILIATIONS
Member, American Accounting Association

PREVIOUS EMPLOYMENT HISTORY
Controller, University of Northern Colorado, Greeley, CO   1974-79

LINDA SUE RUSSO
2198 Mulberry Street
Ft. Collins, CO 80521
(303) 224-2100

OBJECTIVE
Dean, Educational Services

EDUCATION
MA, Education Administration, 1979
University of Northern Colorado, Greeley, CO

BA, Student Personnel, Service, and Counseling, 1974
University of Colorado, Boulder, CO

PROFESSIONAL EXPERIENCE

DEAN, EDUCATIONAL SERVICES   1984-present
Front Range Community College, Ft. Collins, CO
- Direct the planning, development, coordination and implementation of services to meet the goals of the college and needs of the community.

  - Admissions, registration, assessment, special education, supplemental services, counseling, career planning, financial aid offices.

- Coordinate all Educational Services activities with other campuses and sites.

- Oversee the operations of the Library and the operation of the Records Center.

- Responsible for student welfare on campus, including disciplinary procedures and due process in accordance with college guidelines.

COMMUNITY SERVICE
Volunteer, Women's Center, Ft. Collins, CO
Volunteer, United Way of America, Ft. Collins, CO
Volunteer, Larimer County Human Development, Ft. Collins, CO

PREVIOUS EMPLOYMENT HISTORY
Assistant Dean, Student Services, Aims Community College, Greeley, CO 1979-84
Student Personnel Counselor, University of Denver, Denver, CO   1974-79

KEITH C. JENNINGS
3321 Overland Trail Road
Ft. Collins, CO 80521
(303) 224-3218

OBJECTIVE
Director of Human Resources

EDUCATION
MA, Education Administration, 1979
University of Northern Colorado, Greeley, CO

BA, Student Personnel, Service, and Counseling, 1974
University of Denver, Denver, CO

PROFESSIONAL EXPERIENCE

DIRECTOR OF HUMAN RESOURCES   1979-present
Front Range Community College, Ft. Collins, CO
- Direct the Human Resources office consisting of six staff members for a multi-campus college with rapid growth and change, reporting directly to the president of the college.

- Plan, develop, and implement personnel policies and procedures for both classified and nonclassified staff.

- Develop and administer the college recruitment and selection program, employee relations function, affirmative action program, classification, compensation system, and professional development program.

- Administer the benefit program, grievance procedures, performance appraisal system, and maintenance of personnel records and database.

COMMUNITY SERVICE
Board Member, Larimer County Human Development, Ft. Collins, CO
Volunteer, American Red Cross, Ft. Collins, CO

PREVIOUS EMPLOYMENT HISTORY
Assistant Director of Personnel, Aims Community College, Greeley, CO   1974-79

ERNESTINE L. GERALD
2195 Lake Street
Ft. Collins, CO 80521
(303) 224-2136

OBJECTIVE
Director, Literacy Program

EDUCATION
MA, Adult Education, 1979
University of Northern Colorado, Greeley, CO

BA, English Literature, 1974
University of Denver, Denver, CO

PROFESSIONAL EXPERIENCE

LITERACY PROGRAM DIRECTOR   1979-present
Front Range Community College, Ft. Collins, CO
- In charge of overall operations of countrywide literacy programs.

- Supervise staff and schedule classes.

- Monitor federal and state literacy grants to ensure compliance with regard to budget control and grant objectives.

- Direct activities related to volunteer and student recruitment.

- Submit annual grant applications and reports to appropriate agencies.

- Provide leadership and represent the college in literacy matters.

COMMUNITY SERVICE
Board Member, Literacy Programs of America, 1985
Board Member, Colorado Literacy Association, 1984

PREVIOUS EMPLOYMENT HISTORY
Assistant Director/Literacy, University of Northern Colorado, Greeley, CO   1976-79
English Instructor, Aims Community College, Greeley, CO   1974-76

CLAUDE I. HAUF
1957 Forest Green Drive
Ft. Collins, CO 80521
(303) 224-3217

OBJECTIVE
Drafting Instructor

EDUCATION
MA, Education, 1979
University of Northern Colorado, Greeley, CO

BA, Architecture, 1974
University of Denver, Denver, CO

PROFESSIONAL EXPERIENCE

DRAFTING INSTRUCTOR   1979-present
Front Range Community College, Ft. Collins, CO
- Teach courses in drafting, including classes in CAD.

- Develop and upgrade courses in the drafting and CAD areas and develop curriculum content.

- Actively participate in division and college activities and committees while providing leadership in the drafting issues.

- Select textbooks, recommend schedule of classes, budget, and participate in hiring part-time faculty.

COMMUNITY SERVICE/AFFILIATIONS
Member, National Association of Architects
Volunteer, United Way of America, Ft. Collins, CO

PREVIOUS EMPLOYMENT HISTORY
Architect, Johnson & Johnson Architects, Denver, CO   1974-present
Drafting Instructor, Aims Community College, Greeley, CO   1974-79

GEORGE PAUL SAUNDERS
111 Mountain Avenue
Ft. Collins, CO 80524
(303) 224-1117

OBJECTIVE
English Composition Instructor

EDUCATION
MA, English, 1979
University of Northern Colorado, Greeley, CO

BA, English, 1974
University of Denver, Denver, CO

Colorado Teaching Credential, **Philosophy, 1974**

PROFESSIONAL EXPERIENCE

ENGLISH INSTRUCTOR   1979-present
Front Range Community College, Ft. Collins, CO
- Teach courses in English including literature, composition, computerized composition, and research.

- Serve on committees, providing leadership to the English Department and to part-time faculty.

- Develop English programs, new curriculums and select text books.

- Act as educational advisor for the entire English Department.

AFFILIATIONS
Member, National Education Association
Member, Community College Education Association
Member, Colorado Teachers of English Association

PREVIOUS EMPLOYMENT HISTORY
English Instructor, Aims Community College, Greeley, CO   1974-79
Teacher's Aide, University of Denver, Denver, CO   1972-74

GARTH C. JORDAY
874 Riverdale Drive
Ft. Collins, CO 80521
(303) 224-2246

OBJECTIVE
Faculty Chair, Arts and Humanities

EDUCATION
MA, Arts and Humanities, 1979
University of Northern Colorado, Greeley, CO

BA, Education Administration, 1974
University of Denver, Denver, CO

PROFESSIONAL EXPERIENCE

FACULTY CHAIR, ARTS AND HUMANITIES   1979-present
Front Range Community College, Ft. Collins, CO

- Develop and teach new courses in the Arts and Humanities area.

- Produce curriculum content guides.

- Actively participate in division and college activities and committees.

- Serve as faculty chair for Arts and Humanities.

- Develop and monitor budget course schedules and faculty teaching assignments.

- Select and order textbooks.

- Update catalog and provide leadership to department.

- Promote student enjoyment and career participation in the Arts and Humanities.

COMMUNITY SERVICE/AFFILIATIONS
Member, Community College Association for the Arts
Volunteer, United Way of America

PREVIOUS EMPLOYMENT HISTORY
Faculty Chair, Arts/Humanities, Aims Community College, Greeley, CO   1974-79

MARK CHARLES WILHEIM
4310 Lake Forest Drive
Ft. Collins, CO 80521
(303) 224-2132

OBJECTIVE
Forestry, Wildlife, Natural Resources Instructor

EDUCATION
Colorado Vocational Teaching Credential, 1979
University of Northern Colorado, Greeley, CO

BS, Agriculture, 1974
Colorado State University, Ft. Collins, CO

PROFESSIONAL EXPERIENCE

FORESTRY, WILDLIFE, NATURAL RESOURCES INSTRUCTOR   1984-present
Front Range Community College, Ft. Collins, CO
- Teach daily courses in the Forestry, Wildlife, and Natural Resources Program to high school students at the community college.
- Develop course curriculum and advise faculty and staff in the Forestry, Wildlife, and Natural Resources Program.
- Select textbooks for courses offered.
- Serve on committees and provide leadership to part-time faculty.

PROFESSIONAL PROFILE
- Provide strong academic, vocational education, FFA, and Environmental Biotechnology experience.
- Experienced in diverse teaching techniques and appropriate assessment skills.

COMMUNITY SERVICE
Member, Rotary Club, Ft. Collins, CO
Member, Colorado Forestry Service Association

PREVIOUS EMPLOYMENT HISTORY
Forestry Instructor, Aims Community College, Greeley, CO   1979-84
Instructor's Aide, Colorado State University, Ft. Collins, CO   1972-74

WAYNE JASON RUBLE
145 Wagon Wheel Road
Ft. Collins, CO 80521
(303) 224-3387

OBJECTIVE
Driving Instructor position

EDUCATION
MS, Psychology, 1974
University of Northern Colorado, Greeley, CO

BS, Education Administration, 1970
University of Northern Colorado, Greeley, CO

SPECIAL CREDENTIALS
Colorado Teaching Credential, Driver's Education, Life

PROFESSIONAL EXPERIENCE

INSTRUCTOR, DRIVER'S EDUCATION   1974-present
Rocky Mountain High School, Ft. Collins, CO
- Instruct individuals and groups of students in theory and application of automobile driver skills.

- Teach handling automobile emergencies, driving techniques, and mechanical operation using blackboard diagrams, audiovisual aids, and driving simulators.

- Observe individual's driving habits and reactions under various driving conditions to ensure conformance with vehicle operational standards and state vehicle code.

- Test hearing and vision of individuals, using lettered charts and colored lights.

- Teach motor vehicle regulations and insurance laws.

PREVIOUS EMPLOYMENT HISTORY
Driver's Education Instructor, Ft. Collins High School, Ft. Collins, CO   1970-74

JOY ANNA YORK
2213 Taft Hill Road
Ft. Collins, CO 80521
(303) 224-8760

OBJECTIVE
Interim Campus Registrar

EDUCATION
MA, Education Administration, 1979
University of Northern Colorado, Greeley, CO

BA, Education Administration, 1974
University of Denver, Denver, CO

PROFESSIONAL EXPERIENCE

INTERIM CAMPUS REGISTRAR   1979-present
Front Range Community College, Westminster, CO
- Manage the Records Office and the student services of the Registrar.

- Implement the process of student appeals for exemption from deadlines and procedures and the administration of the cost center.

- Participate in curriculum and academic standards committees.

- Oversee maintenance of student records consistent with federal and state regulations; enrollment certifications; technical programs (SIS+, On Course, Classroom Management, etc.); transcripts, and incoming transcript evaluation.

- Participate in Educational Services Administrative Council Activities and college-wide review and drafting of procedures and policies; commencement planning; touch-tone registration planning and spring registration debrief.

- Develop the Schedule of Courses college-wide for three campuses.

PREVIOUS EMPLOYMENT HISTORY
Interim Campus Registrar, Aims Community College, Greeley, CO

JULIE SUE WATSON
320 Laurel Street
Ft. Collins, CO 80524
(303) 498-2219

OBJECTIVE
Interpreter Coordinator

EDUCATION
MA, Speech-Language Pathology, 1979
University of Northern Colorado, Greeley, CO

BA, Special Education, 1974
University of Denver, Denver, CO

Certificate of Clinical Competence (CCC-SP)
American Speech-Language & Health Association (ASHA)

PROFESSIONAL EXPERIENCE

INTERPRETER COORDINATOR   1992-present
Front Range Community College, Ft. Collins, CO
- Provide interpreting and other services to deaf and hearing-impaired students in educational programs while regular interpreter is on sabbatical.
- Coordinate school activities and serve as liaison for hearing-impaired students.

SPEECH-LANGUAGE PATHOLOGIST   1979-present
Poudre Valley Hospital, Ft. Collins, CO
- Perform diagnostic speech and language procedures to outpatient, inpatient, and home care including hearing-impaired adults.
- Develop/administer treatment plans including education for home programs.
- Document evaluations, treatment, progress, and results.
- Develop programs for new services that include protocols, assessment procedures, and treatment programs.
- Promote department services through verbal and written distribution of information and staffing booths.
- Consult with physicians, staff, family members, and patients.
- Participate in in-services, continuing education, and professional reading.
- Coordinate services for interdisciplinary teams.
- Present rounds and inservices for staff and community organizations.

PREVIOUS EMPLOYMENT HISTORY
Speech-Language Pathologist, University of Denver, Denver, CO   1974-79

MARGARET ANNE FROST

432 Lincoln Court
Ft. Collins, CO 80524
(303) 224-1049

OBJECTIVE
Media Specialist

EDUCATION
MLS, Library Science, 1979
University of Northern Colorado, Greeley, CO

BS, Library Science, 1974
University of Denver, Denver, CO

PROFESSIONAL EXPERIENCE

MEDIA SPECIALIST   1979-present
Front Range Community College, Ft. Collins, CO
- Select learning materials by using professional and commercial selection tools and working with faculty, staff, and students.

- Work with the main campus to order learning materials.

- Monitor materials budget account.

- Serve as the main resource person to faculty in determining library needs.

- Answer patron requests for information.

- Offer bibliographic instruction students, faculty, and staff on an individual and/or group basis including library tours, use of specific resources and materials, referrals to outside resources.

- Conduct class orientations on use of the library.

- Work closely with main campus and other libraries to provide interlibrary loan service to patrons.

PREVIOUS EMPLOYMENT HISTORY
Librarian, University of Northern Colorado, Greeley, CO   1976-79
Librarian, Aims Community College, Greeley, CO   1974-76

RICHARD CHARLES JOEL
3212 Lake Street
Ft. Collins, CO 80524
(303) 224-2214

OBJECTIVE
Mathematics Instructor

EDUCATION
MS, Mathematics, 1979
University of Northern Colorado, Greeley, CO

BS, Mathematics, 1974
University of Denver, Denver, CO

CREDENTIALS
Colorado Secondary, **Mathematics, 1974**
Colorado Secondary, **Elementary Education, 1978**

PROFESSIONAL EXPERIENCE

1979-present

Front Range Community College, Ft. Collins, CO
- Teach daily courses in Basic Math, Consumer Math, and College Algebra.
- Develop new course and curriculum content.
- Serve as faculty chair for Mathematics.
- Develop and monitor budget, course schedules, and faculty teaching assignments.
- Select and order textbooks.
- Update catalog and provide leadership to department.

AFFILIATIONS
Member, National Education Association
Member, Poudre Education Association
Member, Colorado Teachers of Mathematics Association

PREVIOUS EMPLOYMENT HISTORY
Mathematics Instructor, Aims Community College, Greeley, CO   1974-79
Teacher's Aide, Centennial High School Denver, CO   1972-74

JOHN WHITFIELD
987 Lake Street
Ft. Collins, CO 80521
(303) 224-3213

OBJECTIVE
Mathematics Instructor

EDUCATION
MS, Math Education, 1976
University of Northern Colorado, Greeley, CO

BS, Mathematics, 1974
University of Denver, Denver, CO

CREDENTIALS
Colorado Secondary Mathematics, 1978
Colorado Elementary Education, 1975

PROFESSIONAL EXPERIENCE

MATHEMATICS INSTRUCTOR   1979-present
Colorado State University, Ft. Collins, CO
- Teach Mathematics courses including Calculus and Statistics using graphics calculators and computers.

- Advise curriculum and program development to Mathematics Department.

- Select textbooks for courses taught.

- Serve on committees and provide leadership to part-time faculty.

AFFILIATIONS
Member, Rotary Club, Ft. Collins, 1979
Member, Community College Mathematics Association

PREVIOUS EMPLOYMENT HISTORY
Mathematics Instructor, Aims Community College, Greeley, CO   1976-79
Instructor's Aide, Front Range Community College, Westminster, CO   1974-76

ROBERT S. SCHULLER
521 Peterson Street
Ft. Collins, CO 80524
(303) 224-2436

OBJECTIVE
Media Specialist

EDUCATION
PhD Library Science, 1974
Colorado State University, Ft. Collins, CO

MLS, Library Administration, 1970
Colorado State University, Ft. Collins, CO

Colorado Secondary Teaching Credential, History, 1970

PROFESSIONAL EXPERIENCE

MEDIA SPECIALIST   1978-present
Ft. Collins High School, Ft. Collins, CO
- Supervise and coordinate the day-to-day media center operations.
- Share information on the latest educational research, trends, methods, materials, and technology with staff.
- Create environment in the media center where everyone feels safe and free from failure.
- Assist teachers in curriculum planning and design and development of instructional strategies leading to integration of media and technologies.
- Interpret district procedures and policies, including the copyright law to staff and students.
- Serve as liaison with other schools, the district media center, the community, and state and national associations.
- Prepare, submit, and administer annual budget allocations and projects for future needs.
- Develop and implement procedures for effective scheduling and use of the media facilities and learning resources.
- Assist in the selection, evaluation, training, delegation of duties, and scheduling for media center support staff, student assistants, and volunteers.
- Consult with the principal and teachers to develop the philosophy, goals, and objects of the school media program.
- Collect data and conduct an ongoing evaluation of the media program in order to determine strengths and areas of improvement.
- Work with the district media program leadership to ensure that the building program is a vital part of a comprehensive, quality district-wide media program.

- More -

PROFESSIONAL PROFILE

- Knowledge and skills in delivering effective instructions.
- Strive to meet the learning needs of all students to enhance their positive self-concept.
- Thorough knowledge of content and teaching methods of History.
- Demonstrate knowledge of developmental needs of students.
- Excellent written and oral communication skills.
- Ability to establish and maintain effective, cooperative relationships with school personnel, students, and parents.
- Demonstrate understanding and empathy necessary for working with students.

AFFILIATIONS

Member, American Librarian Association

PREVIOUS EMPLOYMENT HISTORY

Librarian, Rocky Mountain High, Ft. Collins, CO   1974-78
Teacher, History, Lincoln Junior High, Ft. Collins, CO   1970-74

MARGARET S. MULLINS

221 Whedbee Street
Ft. Collins, CO 80524
(303) 224-2226

OBJECTIVE
Media Specialist

EDUCATION
PhD Library Science, 1974
Colorado State University, Ft. Collins, CO

MLS, Library Administration, 1970
Colorado State University, Ft. Collins, CO

Colorado Secondary Teaching Credential, English, 1970

PROFESSIONAL EXPERIENCE

MEDIA SPECIALIST   1978-present
Lincoln Junior High School, Ft. Collins, CO
- Provide instructional leadership for school program by selecting resources based on school philosophy, curriculum, teaching strategies, and needs of student.
- Assist teachers in curriculum planning and design and development of instructional strategies leading to integration of media and technologies.
- Work with teachers to integrate location, retrieval, and information interpretation skills with subject areas.
- Prepare bibliographies, reserving media, and assisting with reference searches.
- Remain current in the trends of information management and provide leadership in the use of instructional and informational technology.
- Develop and sequence media skills and learning activity with district curriculum.
- Teach skills necessary to access, retrieve, process, and evaluate information.
- Promote literacy and a love of reading; orient students to the media center.
- Teach skills necessary for independent use of media resources.
- Encourage use of a variety of resources and multisensory learning experience in classrooms and in media center to help prepare students for success in the information and technological age and for lifelong learning.
- Lead students in an understanding and appreciation of cultural diversity and our communal stories by providing access to a wide range of literature and media.
- Provide leadership and support in the interdisciplinary use of computers, instructional television, video, telecommunications, and other technologies.
- Participate on district committees and in setting district-level procedures to help ensure that building-level needs of the learning community are met.

- More -

PROFESSIONAL PROFILE
- Knowledge and skills in delivering effective instructions.
- Thorough knowledge of content and teaching methods of English.
- Demonstrate knowledge of developmental needs of students.
- Excellent written and oral communication skills.
- Ability to establish and maintain effective, cooperative relationships with school personnel, students, and parents.
- Demonstrate understanding and empathy necessary for working with students.

AFFILIATIONS
Member, American Librarian Association

PREVIOUS EMPLOYMENT HISTORY
Librarian, Lesher Junior High, Ft. Collins, CO   1974-78
Teacher, English, Rocky Mountain High, Ft. Collins, CO   1970-74

PENELOPE S. DAVID
2214 Smith Street
Ft. Collins, CO 80524
(303) 224-1226

OBJECTIVE
Media Specialist

EDUCATION
PhD Library Science, 1974
Colorado State University, Ft. Collins, CO

MLS, Library Administration, 1970
Colorado State University, Ft. Collins, CO

Colorado Secondary Teaching Credential, English, 1970

PROFESSIONAL EXPERIENCE
MEDIA SPECIALIST   1978-present
Shepardson Elementary School, Ft. Collins, CO
- Provide instructional leadership for school program by selecting resources based on school philosophy, curriculum, teaching strategies, and needs of student.
- Assist teachers in curriculum planning and design and development of instructional strategies leading to integration of media and technologies.
- Work with teachers to integrate location, retrieval, and information interpretation skills with subject areas.
- Prepare bibliographies, reserving media, and assisting with reference searches.
- Remain current in the trends of information management and provide leadership in the use of instructional and informational technology.
- Develop and sequence media skills and learning activity with district curriculum.
- Teach skills necessary to access, retrieve, process, and evaluate information.
- Promote literacy and a love of reading; orient students to the media center.
- Teach skills necessary for independent use of media resources.
- Encourage use of a variety of resources and multisensory learning experience in classrooms and in media center to help prepare students for success in the information and technological age and for lifelong learning.
- Lead students in an understanding and appreciation of cultural diversity and our communal stories by providing access to a wide range of literature and media.
- Provide leadership and support in the interdisciplinary use of computers, instructional television, video, telecommunications, and other technologies.
- Participate on district committees and in setting district-level procedures to help ensure that building-level needs of the learning community are met.

- More -

PROFESSIONAL PROFILE

- Knowledge and skills in delivering effective instructions.
- Thorough knowledge of content and teaching methods of English.
- Demonstrate knowledge of developmental needs of students.
- Excellent written and oral communication skills.
- Ability to establish and maintain effective, cooperative relationships with school personnel, students, and parents.
- Demonstrate understanding and empathy necessary for working with students.

AFFILIATIONS

Member, American Librarian Association

PREVIOUS EMPLOYMENT HISTORY

Librarian, Irish Elementary School, Ft. Collins, CO   1974-78
Teacher, English, Lesher Junior High, Ft. Collins, CO   1970-74

RACHEL S. SIMPSON
3214 Lake Forest Drive
Ft. Collins, CO 80521
(303) 224-2213

OBJECTIVE
Nursing Instructor

EDUCATION
Registered Nurse, State of Colorado, 1974

MS, Nursing, 1979
Colorado State University, Ft. Collins, CO

BS, Nursing, 1974
University of Denver, Denver, CO

PROFESSIONAL EXPERIENCE

NURSING INSTRUCTOR   1979-present
Front Range Community College, Ft. Collins, CO
- Teach postsecondary courses including Fundamentals of Nursing, Medical-Surgical Nursing, Pediatric Nursing, and Pharmacology.

- Supervise students in clinical settings.

- Serve as advisor to staff members and participate on committees.

- Recruit nursing students.

COMMUNITY SERVICE/AFFILIATIONS
Member, Hospice Inc. of Larimer County
Member, American Red Cross, Ft. Collins, CO
Volunteer, Women's Center, Ft. Collins, CO

PREVIOUS EMPLOYMENT HISTORY
Registered Nurse, Poudre Valley Hospital, Ft. Collins, CO   1974-79

BONNIE B. GARROTTE
2213 Lake Street
Ft. Collins, CO 80521
(303) 224-2213

OBJECTIVE
Philosophy Instructor

EDUCATION
MA, Philosophy, 1979
University of Northern Colorado, Greeley, CO

BA, Philosophy, 1974
University of Denver, Denver, CO

Colorado Teaching Credential, **Philosophy, 1974**

PROFESSIONAL EXPERIENCE

PHILOSOPHY INSTRUCTOR   1979-present
Front Range Community College, Ft. Collins, CO
- Teach a full course load in Philosophy on a daily basis in the Humanities Department.

- Serve as student advisor for the college's Philosophy Club, demonstrating commitment to diversity, ethics, and teaching excellence.

- Contribute to Humanities Department, campus and college activities and initiatives including: advising, curriculum and program development, selecting textbooks, serving on committees, and providing leadership to adjunct faculty.

AFFILIATIONS
Member, National Education Association
Member, Community College Education Association
Member, Colorado Teachers of Philosophy Association

PREVIOUS EMPLOYMENT HISTORY
Philosophy Instructor, Aims Community College, Greeley, CO   1974-79
Teacher's Aide, University of Denver, Denver, CO   1972-74

LEROY S. SUMMERVILLE
112 Terry Shores Road
Ft. Collins, CO 80524
(303) 224-2832

OBJECTIVE
High School Principal position

EDUCATION
MEA, Education Administration, 1974
University of Northern Colorado, Greeley, CO

BA, Sociology, 1970
University of Northern Colorado, Greeley, CO

CERTIFICATION
Colorado Secondary, Elementary Education, 1974

PROFESSIONAL EXPERIENCE
PRINCIPAL   1978-present
Rocky Mountain High School, Ft. Collins, CO
- Direct and coordinate educational, administrative, and counseling activities.
- Develop and evaluate educational program to ensure conformance to state and school board standards.
- Develop and administer educational programs for students with mental or physical handicaps.
- Develop and coordinate educational programs through meetings with staff, review of teachers' activities, and issuance of directives.
- Confer with teachers, students, and parents concerning educational and behavioral problems in school.
- Establish and maintain relationships with colleges, community organizations, and other schools to coordinate educational services.
- Requisition and allocate supplies, equipment, and instructional material.
- Direct preparation of class schedules, cumulative records/attendance reports.
- Observe and evaluate teacher performance; interview and hire teachers.
- Monitor safety and security; plan and monitor school budget.

COMMUNITY RELATIONS
Social Chair, Rotary Club, Ft. Collins, CO, since 1974

PREVIOUS EMPLOYMENT HISTORY
Assistant Principal, Ft. Collins High School, Ft. Collins, CO   1974-78

ANNA MARIE PAULETTE
224 Franklin Street
Ft. Collins, CO 80524
(303) 224-0226

OBJECTIVE
Psychologist

EDUCATION
MS, Psychology, 1974
Colorado State University, Ft. Collins, CO

BS, Psychology, 1970
University of Colorado, Boulder, CO

Colorado Secondary Teaching Credential, Psychology, 1970

PROFESSIONAL EXPERIENCE

PSYCHOLOGY   1974-present
Lincoln Junior High School, Ft. Collins, CO
- Complete due process parental counseling and make requests for surrogate parent when appropriate.
- Assist in developing and selecting individual strategies and materials for Individualized Education Program (IEP).
- Help prescribe appropriate annual goals and short-term objectives.
- Assist in translating IEP goals/objectives into specific sequences of intervention.
- Assist teachers in mainstreaming strategies, modification of teaching environment, curriculum, and coordinating information with other agencies.
- Complete information necessary for district special education records as required by state and federal agencies.
- Educate parents or guardians of their rights and due process.
- Assist parents or guardians in understanding team recommendations and allow them to express their opinions with consideration.
- Interview child when deemed necessary, report any child abuse to principal, and file written report on Poudre R-1 form and send it to Social Services.
- Provide in-service training in area of child abuse for all teachers and staff for schools in the district, meeting deadline schedules.
- Serve as model for students, showing effort and enthusiasm for learning.
- Encourage expression of respect for one another, self-pride, and success.
- Participate in staff development activities, continuing education courses and professional organizations remaining current regarding ideas and methods.

- More -

PROFESSIONAL EXPERIENCE (Continued)

- Provide direct consultation to parents/guardians on intervention strategies for dealing with student; promote parent interest in school activities.
- Offer assistance for resolving problems within the school environment and assist administrators in redefining school procedures and resolving issues.
- Initiate and support ideas that contribute to the excellence of building and district programs; participate in cooperative planning with colleagues.
- Make referrals to and consult with other appropriate agencies.
- Recognize hazardous situations and act on them.
- Report any information involving danger to the health and safety of the child.

PROFESSIONAL PROFILE

- Ability to establish and maintain effective, cooperative relationships with school personnel, students, and parents.
- Excellent written and oral communication skills.
- Adhere to National and State ethical standards for social workers.
- Follow Board of Education policies.
- Demonstrate a concern for student health and safety.

AFFILIATIONS
Member, American Social Workers Association
Member, North Central Association

PREVIOUS EMPLOYMENT HISTORY
Psychologist, Blevins Junior High School, Ft. Collins, CO   1970-74

MARIANNE S. COLLIER
442 Peterson Street
Ft. Collins, CO 80524
(303) 224-6526

OBJECTIVE
School Nurse

EDUCATION
BS, Nursing, 1970
Colorado State University, Ft. Collins, CO

Critical Care Nursing Certificate, 1970
Front Range Community College, Ft. Collins, CO

Colorado Secondary Teaching Credential, Nursing, 1970

PROFESSIONAL EXPERIENCE

SCHOOL NURSE 1974-present
Rocky Mountain High School, Ft. Collins, CO

- Observe and monitor behaviors symptomatic of changes in health status, and environmental conditions that may present health hazards.

- Assess physical status to determine current health needs, including developing a database from student's health history and medical records.

- Participate as a member of an interdisciplinary team to provide anticipatory guidance toward health goals, and interpret stages of developmental process.

- Assist in setting priorities consistent with student and family needs.

- Maintain health records, medication schedules, progress notes for students.

- Complete a Health Care Action Plan when appropriate.

- Implement physical assessment and provide primary care for students including treatment, emergency care, referrals to other professionals.

- Provide health education for parents, students, staff, and volunteers.

- Assess individual student's position on wellness continuum, activity tolerance, nutritional status, and adaptive behaviors.

- More -

PROFESSIONAL EXPERIENCE (Continued)

- Establish screening programs for various health problems, i.e., (vision, hearing, dental, scoliosis, and communicable disease), according to accepted standards.

- Function as part of an educational team in the development of the IEP.

PROFESSIONAL PROFILE

- Serve as a member of the school Staffing Team and follow Due Process Procedures.

- Possess knowledge of developmental needs of students.

- Work with students with empathy and understanding.

- Ability to establish and maintain effective, cooperative relationships with school personnel, students, and parents.

- Maintain excellent written and oral communication skills.

AFFILIATIONS
Member, American Nurses Association
Member, Educational Nurses Association

PREVIOUS EMPLOYMENT HISTORY
School Nurse, Ft. Collins High School, Ft. Collins, CO   1970-74

NINA O. RUBINS
112 Oak Street
Ft. Collins, CO 80524
(303) 224-1926

OBJECTIVE
School Nurse

EDUCATION
BS, Nursing, 1970
Colorado State University, Ft. Collins, CO

Special Education Certificate, 1970
Front Range Community College, Ft. Collins, CO

Colorado Secondary Teaching Credential, Nursing, 1970

PROFESSIONAL EXPERIENCE

SCHOOL NURSE   1974-present
Irish Elementary School, Ft. Collins, CO
- Identify health needs of students, formulate a plan of health care, and implement health care services, providing primary care for students.

- Assess individual student's position on wellness continuum, activity tolerance, nutritional status, and adaptive behaviors.

- Assist in the identification and programming for handicapped students with special needs.

- Function as part of an educational team in the developing the Individualized Education Program (IEP).

- Plan intervention consistent with the Individual Education Program.

- Refer students for evaluation or therapy.

- Interpret professionals' and agency reports and school reports to school staff and parents.

- Work with staff and other support staff to maximize the developmental potential, and effectiveness of the school experience for each student.

- More -

PROFESSIONAL EXPERIENCE (Continued)
- Identify family health-related needs and provide counseling for student's immediate family and primary caretakers.

- Establish screening programs for various health problems, (vision, hearing, dental, scoliosis, and communicable disease), according to accepted standards.

PROFESSIONAL PROFILE
- Serve as a member of the school Staffing Team and follow Due Process Procedures.

- Possess knowledge of developmental needs of students.

- Work with students with empathy and understanding.

- Ability to establish and maintain effective, cooperative relationships with school personnel, students, and parents.

- Maintain excellent written and oral communication skills.

AFFILIATIONS
Member, American Nurses Association
Member, Special Educational Nurses Association

PREVIOUS EMPLOYMENT HISTORY
School Nurse, Shepardson Elementary School, Ft. Collins, CO   1972-74
School Nurse, Barton Elementary School, Ft. Collins, CO   1970-72

GLENN ROBERT MOSS

214 Loomis Street
Ft. Collins, CO 80524
(303) 224-2213

OBJECTIVE
Social Sciences Instructor

EDUCATION
MA, Social Sciences, 1979
University of Northern Colorado, Greeley, CO

BA, Social Sciences, 1974
University of Denver, Denver, CO

Credential: Colorado Community College, Social Science, 1974

PROFESSIONAL EXPERIENCE

SOCIAL SCIENCE INSTRUCTOR   1979-present
Front Range Community College, Ft. Collins, CO
- Teach daily courses in the Social Sciences.

- Develop new courses and curriculum content in Social Sciences.

- Actively participate in division and college activities and committees and serve as faculty chair for Social Sciences.

- Develop and monitor budget, course schedules, faculty teaching assignments.

- Select and order textbooks.

- Update catalog and provide leadership to the department.

AFFILIATIONS
Member, National Education Association
Member, Colorado Teachers of Social Sciences Association
Member, Community College Education Association

PREVIOUS EMPLOYMENT HISTORY
Social Sciences Instructor, Aims Community College, Greeley, CO   1974-79

JORDAN PAUL DUGGINS
102 Peterson Street
Ft. Collins, CO 80524
(303) 224-0526

OBJECTIVE
Social Worker

EDUCATION
MS, Sociology, 1974
Colorado State University, Ft. Collins, CO

BS, Psychology, 1970
University of Colorado, Boulder, CO

Colorado Secondary Teaching Credential, Social Worker, 1970

PROFESSIONAL EXPERIENCE
SOCIAL WORKER   1974-present
Rocky Mountain High School, Ft. Collins, CO
- Assist in the identification and programming for handicapped students.
- Plan and implement intervention consistent with the Individualized Educational Program (IEP).
- Provide ongoing consultation services to staff.
- Allocate appropriate time for assessment planning and intervention.
- Make referrals to and consult with other appropriate agencies.
- Communicate effectively with students and provide frequent feedback.
- Provide direct services to specified students to meet social-emotional needs.
- Give direct service/consultation to parents or guardians on intervention strategies for dealing with the student.
- Present information on handicapping condition, prognosis, intervention, impact of labels, issues, and support for family.
- Contribute to maintaining necessary student records.
- Facilitate special education meetings with parents or guardians and staff.
- Follow mandated guidelines in reporting child abuse and neglect.
- Provide in service training in child abuse.
- Assist in establishing clear expectations for appropriate student behavior.
- Participate in staff development activities, continuing education courses and professional organizations.
- Recognize problems and actively contribute to the resolution at the Department of Special Education or Building Level.
- Collaborate with others to fulfill responsibilities related to building and district goals and priorities.

- More -

PROFESSIONAL PROFILE
- Ability to establish and maintain effective, cooperative relationships with school personnel, students, and parents.
- Excellent written and oral communication skills.
- Adhere to National and State ethical standards for social workers.
- Follow Board of Education policies.
- Demonstrate a concern for student health and safety.

AFFILIATIONS
Member, <u>American Social Workers Association</u>
Member, <u>North Central Association</u>

PREVIOUS EMPLOYMENT HISTORY
Social Worker, <u>Ft. Collins High School</u>, Ft. Collins, CO   1970-74

JODELL S. RIES
332 Sheeley Drive
Ft. Collins, CO 80524
(303) 224-5540

OBJECTIVE
Special Education Supervisor

EDUCATION
MA, Special Education, 1974
University of Northern Colorado, Greeley, CO

BA, Special Education, 1970
University of Northern Colorado, Greeley, CO

SPECIAL TRAINING
Learning Handicapped Specialist Teaching Credential, Life
Single Subject Teaching Credential, English, Life

PROFESSIONAL EXPERIENCE

SUPERVISOR, SPECIAL EDUCATION   **1982-present**
Poudre R-1 School District, Ft. Collins, CO
- Direct and coordinate activities of teachers and staff providing home or school instruction, evaluation services, job placement, and other services to physically, mentally, emotionally, or neurologically handicapped children.
- Review referrals and diagnose and participate in conferences with administrators, staff, parents, children, and other concerned parties to formulate recommendations for student placement and provision of services.
- Monitor staff activities and give technical assistance in assessment, curriculum development, materials and equipment use, and management of student behavior.
- Plan and conduct in-service training.
- Interview applicants, recommend hirings, and evaluate staff performance.
- Write grant proposals and assist program administrators in preparing budget and developing program policy and goals.
- Address public to elicit support and explain program objectives.

PROFESSIONAL AFFILIATIONS
- Association for Children and Adults with Learning Disabilities (ACALD) - Ft. Collins, CO, since 1974
- Council on Exceptional Children - Early Childhood Division

MARIANNE RENEE PAISLEY
1690 Horsetooth Drive
Ft. Collins, CO 80525
(303) 225-0059

OBJECTIVE
Special Education Director

EDUCATION
MA, Special Education, 1974
University of Northern Colorado, Greeley, CO

BA, Special Education, 1970
University of Northern Colorado, Greeley, CO

SPECIAL TRAINING
Learning Handicapped Specialist Teaching Credential, Life
Single Subject Teaching Credential, English, Life

PROFESSIONAL EXPERIENCE
DIRECTOR, SPECIAL EDUCATION   **1982-present**
Poudre R-1 School District, Ft. Collins, CO
- Direct and coordinate special education programs for Poudre R-1 School District to integrate and teach students with mental or physical disabilities.
- Formulate policies and procedures for new or revised integrated programs and activities, such as screening, placement, education, and training of students.
- Evaluate special education programs to ensure that objectives for each individual student's education are met.
- Interpret laws, rules, and regulations to students, parents, and staff.
- Recruit, select, and evaluate staff.
- Prepare budget and solicit funds to provide financial support for programs.
- Prepare reports for federal, state, and local regulatory agencies.
- Contract with agencies for needed services.

PROFESSIONAL AFFILIATIONS
- Association for Children and Adults with Learning Disabilities (ACALD) - Ft. Collins, CO, since 1974
- Council on Exceptional Children - Early Childhood Division

PREVIOUS EMPLOYMENT HISTORY
Special Ed. Supervisor, Rocky Mountain High School, Ft. Collins, CO   1978-82
Special Ed. Coordinator, Lincoln Junior High School, Ft. Collins, CO   1974-78

TIFFANY R. ASHLEY
345 Peterson Street
Ft. Collins, CO 80524
(303) 224-0026

OBJECTIVE
Speech-Language Specialist

EDUCATION
MS, Speech-Language Pathology, 1974
Colorado State University, Ft. Collins, CO

Certificate of Clinical Competence (CCC-SP), 1970
American Speech-Language & Health Association (ASHA)

Colorado Secondary Teaching Credential, Speech-Language, 1970

PROFESSIONAL EXPERIENCE

SPEECH-LANGUAGE SPECIALIST   1974-present
Lincoln Junior High School, Ft. Collins, CO
- Work with students one-on-one and in group sessions.
- Participate in the identification of programming for handicapped students using formal and informal methods of evaluation.
- Write clear and concise diagnostic results.
- Develop individual long-term goals and short-term objectives based on identifiable needs; use time effectively.
- Use methods that are appropriate for the learner to obtain the goals and objectives as identified on the Individualized Educational Program (IEP).
- Demonstrate instructional flexibility to meet immediate student needs.
- Provide for and maintain student involvement during instruction; communicate effectively with students.
- Use effective reinforcement, retention, and transfer strategies.
- Provide ongoing consultative services to staff members.
- Use student performance and evaluation to monitor the effectiveness of instruction to obtain IEP objectives.
- Effectively communicate student progress to student and associated adults; maintain current levels of student's progress and necessary student records.
- Establish clear expectation for appropriate behavior and demonstrate positive responses to expected behaviors.
- Initiate consequences for inappropriate behaviors.

- More -

PROFESSIONAL EXPERIENCE (Continued)

- Establish a learning environment that encourages development of a positive self-concept and attitude toward learning.
- Provide opportunities for the student to exercise responsibility, independence, honesty, and leadership.
- Convey enjoyment and enthusiasm for teaching; serve as a positive role model in school environment.
- Serve as a member of Staffing Team.
- Establish ongoing communication with teachers and parents.

PROFESSIONAL PROFILE

- Participate in professional growth opportunities to remain current in methods and developments.
- Recognize problems and actively contribute to their resolution.
- Demonstrate concern for students' health and safety.
- Adhere to code of ethics for ASHA, the State of Colorado, and maintain student confidentiality.
- Accept and fulfill assignments in a prompt and efficient manner.
- Follow state and federal special education laws and guidelines as interpreted by the district director of special education.

AFFILIATIONS

Member, American Speech-Language & Health Association
Member, North Central Association

PREVIOUS EMPLOYMENT HISTORY

Speech-Language Specialist, Blevins Junior High School, Ft. Collins, CO   1970-74

MICHAEL STEVEN BRINKLEY
9 North County Road
Ft. Collins, CO 80524
(303) 224-2202

OBJECTIVE
School Superintendent

EDUCATION
MEA, Education Administration, 1974
University of Northern Colorado, Greeley, CO

BA, Personnel Management, 1970
University of Northern Colorado, Greeley, CO

CERTIFICATION
Colorado Secondary, Elementary Education, 1974

PROFESSIONAL EXPERIENCE

SCHOOL SUPERINTENDENT, Larimer County   1978-present
Poudre R-1 School District, Ft. Collins, CO
- Direct and coordinate activities concerned with administration of city and county issues in accordance with board of education standards.
- Formulate plans and policies for educational program and submit them to school board for approval.
- Administer program for selection of school sites, construction of buildings, and provision of equipment and supplies.
- Direct preparation and presentation of school budget and determine amount of school bond issues required to finance educational program.
- Address community and civic groups to enlist their support.
- Interpret program and policies of school system to school personnel, to individuals and community groups, and to governmental agencies.
- Coordinate work of school system with related activities of other districts and agencies.
- Ensure that laws applying to attendance of children at school are enforced.
- Supervise examining, appointing, training, and promotion of teaching personnel.

COMMUNITY RELATIONS
Treasurer, Rotary Club, Ft. Collins, CO, since 1974

PAMELA JOAN LUCILLE
2190 Overland Trail Road
Ft. Collins, CO 80521
(303) 224-1109

OBJECTIVE
Adventure Education Teacher

EDUCATION
MS, Physical Education, 1974
University of Northern Colorado, Greeley, CO

BS, Physical Education, 1970
University of Northern Colorado, Greeley, CO

SPECIAL CREDENTIALS
Colorado Teaching Credential, Physical Education, Life

COMMUNITY SERVICE
Leader, Girl Scouts of America

PROFESSIONAL EXPERIENCE

TEACHER, ADVENTURE EDUCATION   1974-present
Front Range Community College, Ft. Collins, CO

- Instruct and lead students in variety of challenging activities, including rock climbing, canoeing, and skiing to build confidence and promote physical, mental, and social development.

- Appraise students' tolerance to stress. Select and structure learning environment that provides for success in activities appropriate to maturity, interest, and ability.

- Demonstrate basic skills, safety precautions, and other techniques to prepare students for activities.

- Arrange for transportation, food, and equipment for field trips.

- Teach camping and related outdoor skills to students, staff, and volunteers.

PREVIOUS EMPLOYMENT HISTORY
Teacher, Adventure Education, Aims Community College, Greeley, CO   1970-74

CYNTHIA ROBIN MAX
2027 Mathews Street
Ft. Collins, CO 80524
(303) 224-8721

Objective: Art Teacher

EDUCATION
BA, Visual Arts, 1979
Colorado State University, Ft. Collins, CO

Teacher's Certification Program, 1974
University of Northern Colorado, Greeley, CO

CREDENTIALS
Colorado Secondary, **Visual Arts, 1974**
Colorado Secondary, **Elementary Education, 1974**

PROFESSIONAL EXPERIENCE
ART TEACHER   1974-present
Ft. Collins High School, Poudre R-1 School District, Ft. Collins, CO
- Teach Commercial Art and Pottery classes to students, Grades 10-12.

Commercial Art
- Teach students about techniques, equipment, materials, and the media used in Graphic Design.
- Present students with a wide variety of graphic design problems to solve such as Corporate Identity, Typography, Poster Design, Illustration, Book Cover Illustration, and Magazine Layouts.
- Students learn to explore the creative approach to design problem solving using airbrushing, spray painting, painting, pen and ink, cut paper as well as experimenting with multimedia.

Pottery
- Teach students the techniques of hand-building and "throwing" on the potter's wheel utilized in pottery construction.
- Expose students to native cultural influences in pottery design.
- Students learn how to load and fire the kiln, mix glazes, and work on experimental projects.

2-D Design and 3-D Design
- Teach students the importance of a strong foundation in the Art Elements, through the use of 2- and 3-dimensional art media.
- Students learn how to find creative solutions to visual problems.

WOODY S. STAR
907 Mathews Street
Ft. Collins, CO 80524
(303) 224-2221

Objective: Art Teacher

EDUCATION
BA, Visual Arts, 1979
Colorado State University, Ft. Collins, CO

Teacher's Certification Program, 1974
University of Northern Colorado, Greeley, CO

CREDENTIALS
Colorado Secondary, **Visual Arts, 1974**
Colorado Secondary, **Elementary Education, 1974**

PROFESSIONAL EXPERIENCE
ART TEACHER   1974-present
Rocky Mountain High School, Poudre R-1 School District, Ft. Collins, CO
- Teach Drawing and Painting classes to students, Grades 10-12.

Drawing and Advanced Drawing
- Provide opportunity for students to improve their drawing skills while encouraging them to think and express themselves creatively.
- Students explore the use of a variety of techniques and media such as pencil, conte, charcoal, markers, pen and ink, and pastels.
- Students are encouraged to express themselves in a visually creative manner, working with oil pastels, colored pencil, and silk screen in Advanced Drawing.

Painting and Advanced Painting
- Teach students about the basic materials and methods of painting in watercolor and tempera.
- Emphasis is on understanding color relationships, creative expressions, and recognizing the impact of our artistic heritage.
- In Advanced Painting, students are encouraged to take a creative approach in using a wide range of painting styles and techniques.
- Students learn to stretch canvas and work with tempera and acrylic.

2-D Design and 3-D Design
- Teach students the importance of a strong foundation in the Art Elements, through the use of 2- and 3-dimensional art media.
- Students learn how to find creative solutions to visual problems.

SUZANNE A. CROSS
111 Stuart Street
Ft. Collins, CO 80524
(303) 224-3321

Objective: Art Teacher

EDUCATION
BA, Fine Arts, 1979
Colorado State University, Ft. Collins, CO

Teacher's Certification Program, 1974
University of Northern Colorado, Greeley, CO

CREDENTIALS
Colorado Secondary, **Fine Arts, 1974**
Colorado Secondary, **Elementary Education, 1974**

PROFESSIONAL EXPERIENCE
ART TEACHER   1974-present
Lesher Junior High School, Poudre R-1 School District, Ft. Collins, CO
• Teach art classes to students, Grades 7-9.

Art Appreciation and Art I, II, III
• Instruct students on the elements of art and the principles of design.
• Teach classes designed to increase students knowledge of art media, techniques, terminology, and appreciation of aesthetics and art styles in Art I.
  - Emphasize critical thinking skills as students do drawings, paintings, sculpture, printmaking, ceramics, fiber projects, and computer graphics.
• Develop student creative ideas and interests with a greater emphasis on art aesthetics and critical evaluation in Art II.
  - Introduce students to new art concepts, art history, media, and techniques.
• Encourage students to concentrate in areas of special interest to them on major projects in Art III.
  - Introduce new techniques and media such as advanced water color, acrylic painting, mixed media drawings, embossing, multicolor silk screen printing, soft sculpture, casting techniques, batik, fiber arts, airbrush, papermaking, and computer graphics.

Crafts I, II
• Teach students how to design and create functional hand-crafted products including clay, wood, leather, plastics, beading, fibers, metal, and printmaking.
• Educate students on how to develop practical ideas with emphasis on function.
• Study the history and culture of crafts.

CRAIG RANDOLPH SAUL
3214 Mathews Street
Ft. Collins, CO 80524
(303) 224-1121

Objective: Art Teacher

EDUCATION
BA, Photography, 1979
Colorado State University, Ft. Collins, CO

Teacher's Certification Program, 1974
University of Northern Colorado, Greeley, CO

CREDENTIALS
Colorado/California Secondary, Fine Arts, 1974
Colorado/California Secondary, Elementary Education, 1974

PROFESSIONAL EXPERIENCE

ART/PHOTOGRAPHY TEACHER   1979-present
Webber Junior High School, Poudre R-1 School District, Ft. Collins, CO
• Teach photography classes in the Art Department to students, Grades 7-9.

Photography I, II
• Teach students the basic and fundamental use of the 35mm camera.
• Instruct students on darkroom techniques while they participate in the darkroom learning how to develop black and white film, print and enlarge pictures.
• Introduce the history of photography to students.
• Students learn to study the science of photographic chemicals and visual perception is stressed by looking with discrimination through the lens of a camera.
• Photography II is designed to further explore photography.

Crafts I, II
• Teach students how to design and create hand-crafted products with clay, wood, leather, plastics, beading, fibers, metal and printmaking.
• Study the history and culture of crafts.

PREVIOUS EMPLOYMENT HISTORY
Art Teacher, Goleta Union School District, Goleta, CA   1974-79

SUSAN J. DWORSKI
124 Kova Lane
Santa Barbara, CA 93109
(805) 962-2222

Objective: Bilingual Elementary School Teacher

EDUCATION

University of California, Santa Barbara, CA
Bachelor of Arts, Psychology
Graduated with honors, June 1983

Special Courses
Social and Cognitive Development, Language Development, Psychological Issues of the Chicano Child, Independent Research, Bilingual Development and Migrant Children, Masters Course in Special Education.

**TEACHING
CREDENTIAL**

California Multiple Subject Credential Bilingual/ Cross Cultural Emphasis English - Spanish
University of California, Santa Barbara, CA

**FOREIGN
STUDY**

Secundaria del Colegio Guadalupano
Romita, Guanajuato, Mexico, 1972

**TEACHING
EXPERIENCE**

1985-91   **Bilingual Elementary Teacher**
Adams School, Santa Barbara, California
Taught 1st grade and 4th-6th grade after-school Spanish classes.

1985-88   **Bilingual Migrant Teacher**
Migrant Summer School Program, Santa Barbara, California
Taught K-1, Grades 1-3.

1984-85   **Student Teacher**
Carpinteria School District, Carpinteria, California
Taught 3rd grade at the Aliso School. Responsible for teaching Reading (English and Spanish), Math, ESL, Physical Education, and Science.

CHARLES S. OVERTON
2546 Overland Trail
Ft. Collins, CO 80521
(303) 223-2230

OBJECTIVE
Business Education Teacher

EDUCATION
BS, Computer Science, 1979
Colorado State University, Ft. Collins, CO

Teacher's Certification Program, 1974
University of Northern Colorado, Greeley, CO

CREDENTIALS
Colorado Secondary, Business Education, 1974
Colorado Secondary, Elementary Education, 1974

PROFESSIONAL EXPERIENCE

BUSINESS EDUCATION TEACHER   1974-present
Lincoln Junior High School, Poudre R-1 School District, Ft. Collins, CO
- Teach Computer I-III courses to students, Grades 7-9.

Computer I
- Students learn word-processing keyboarding skills including creating, saving, retrieving, spell checking and printing document files.
- Teach students introduction to proofreading and editing.

Computer II
- Instruct how to compose journal entries, letters, essays, and researched reports.
- Desktop publishing fonts and graphics are used to create greeting cards, posters, and letterheads.
- Students learn database entry, mathematical formulas that add, subtract, multiply, divide, and average.

Computer III
- Teach students how to categorize and classify ideas and information through oral and written reports/ presentations.
- Teach students how to critique and analyze advertising used to create videotaped TV/radio commercials, and desktop published flyers, posters, and newspaper ads strengthening higher level thinking, basic communication, and computer skills.

DIANA HOFTMAN
129 Monroe Street
Ft. Collins, CO 80526
(303) 224-9909

OBJECTIVE
Emotionally Impaired Teacher position

EDUCATION
MA, Special Education, 1974
University of Northern Colorado, Greeley, CO

BA, Special Education, 1970
University of California, Santa Barbara, CA

SPECIAL CREDENTIALS
Learning Handicapped Specialist Teaching Credential, Life
Multiple Subject Teaching Credential, K-12, Life
Certified by the county, state and federal government

PROFESSIONAL EXPERIENCE
TEACHER, EMOTIONALLY IMPAIRED   1974-present
Poudre R-1 School District, Ft. Collins, CO
- Teach elementary and secondary school subjects to students with emotional impairments in the Poudre R-1 School District.
- Plan curriculum and prepare lessons to meet individual needs of students, considering their physical, emotional, and educational levels of development.
- Confer with parents, administrator, testing specialists, social worker, and others to develop individual educational program for students.
- Instruct students in academic subject areas and social interaction skills.
- Observe students for signs of disruptive behavior, such as violence, verbal outbursts, and episodes of destructiveness.
- Teach socially acceptable behavior employing techniques such as behavior modification and positive reinforcement.
- Confer with staff members to plan programs designed to promote educational, physical, and social development of students.

PROFESSIONAL AFFILIATIONS
Council on Exceptional Children - Mental Retardation Division

PREVIOUS EMPLOYMENT HISTORY
Teacher, Emotionally Impaired, Goleta Valley School District, Goleta, CA   1970-74

BRIE S. OLYMPIA
210 Lakewood Street
Ventura, CA 93004
(805) 647-0139

OBJECTIVE
High School Teacher

EDUCATION
Multiple Subject Teaching Credential, 1989
University of California, Santa Barbara, CA, GPA: 4.0

BA, English/Art History, 1989
University of California, Santa Barbara, CA

SPECIAL TRAINING
Participated in an intensive 10-week training program at ISP, Peace Crops Training Center in Bukavu, Kivu, Zaire. Included in the subjects studied were intensive French, intensive Tshiluba, TEFL (teaching English as a foreign language), teacher training and cross-cultural training. Attended annual in-service training programs in TEFL methodology.

TEACHING EXPERIENCE

ENGLISH/ART HISTORY TEACHER (Grade 11-12)   1989-94
Peace Corps, Zaire, Africa (Department of National Education)
- Taught 11th and 12th grade English for as many as 120 children and Art History to 60 students.
- Taught Anglo-American Literature to college students at Kananga Teacher's College and served as Director for five students' senior theses.
- Calculated grading and organized lessons on an annual basis.
- Counseled students as Homeroom teacher.
- Coordinated special after-school projects that included arts and crafts, photography, drama, and classes in birth control.
- Helped students to conduct their own lectures.
- Led and participated in staff meetings.
- Tutored Zairian doctors in the English language on a weekly basis.

- More -

SPECIAL SKILLS/EXPERIENCES

- Speak, read, and write fluent French and Tshiluba (African dialect).
- Tutored a Laotian family at the University of California at Santa Barbara in English and helped them to adapt to the American culture.
- Volunteered at the University of California at Santa Barbara Art Museum, organizing receptions and greeting visitors.

AFFILIATIONS
Member, American Teachers Association

LOCATION OF PLACEMENT PAPERS
Educational Careers
Counseling and Career Services
University of California at Santa Barbara
Santa Barbara, CA 93106
(805) 961-4416

RHONDA SUE READ
1200 Overland Trail
Ft. Collins, CO 80521
(303) 224-2130

Objective: English Teacher

EDUCATION
BA, English, 1979
Colorado State University, Ft. Collins, CO

Teacher's Certification Program, 1974
University of Northern Colorado, Greeley, CO

CREDENTIALS
Colorado Secondary, **Language Arts, 1974**
Colorado Secondary, **Elementary Education, 1974**

PROFESSIONAL EXPERIENCE
ENGLISH TEACHER   1974-present
Boltz Junior High School, Poudre R-1 School District, Ft. Collins, CO
• Teach English courses in the Language Arts Department to students, Grades 7-9.

English 7, 8, 9
• Teach students to express themselves more easily and effectively through writing and speaking in English 7.
  - Students study the fundamentals of grammar, correct usage, literature (short stories and novels), the writing process (narration, description, and exposition.
  - Teach how to focus on writing a unified, coherent paragraph that logically supports a topic sentence by using specific details and creative writing.
• Instruct students on how to develop communication and thinking skills through integrated study of language, literature, and writing in English 8.
  - Language study emphasizes sentence patterns, punctuation, spelling, vocabulary, and usage.
  - Writing process focuses on further development of skills and working with multiparagraph writings in narrative, descriptive, and expository writing.
  - Literature studies include the genre or thematic approach, stressing an understanding of literary terminology and author's purpose.
• Teach students effective writing and speaking communication in English 9.
  - This includes levels of usage, the mechanics necessary in writing, proofreading techniques, and introduction to complex sentence patterns.
  - Writing process emphasizes exposition and organization, clarity, and power of expression including evaluation and revision, library skills, and notetaking.
  - Literature focuses on short stories, novels, and play conception.

ASHLEIGH S. LINDSEY
112 Country Club Road
Ft. Collins, CO 80524
(303) 224-2230

Objective: Family Studies Teacher

EDUCATION
BA, Sociology/Psychology, 1979
Colorado State University, Ft. Collins, CO

Teacher's Certification Program, 1974
University of Northern Colorado, Greeley, CO

CREDENTIALS
Colorado Secondary, Psychology/Sociology, 1974
Colorado Secondary, Elementary Education, 1974

PROFESSIONAL EXPERIENCE

FAMILY STUDIES TEACHER   1974-present
Ft. Collins High School, Poudre R-1 School District, Ft. Collins, CO
• Teach Consumer and Family Studies to students Grades 10-12.

Child Psychology and Development
• Teach students who might be interested in a career in child development basic background information and an understanding that parenting is a choice.
• Help students understand child development in the areas of physical, emotional, social, and intellectual development.
• Discuss Children, Parenting and You, Pregnancy and Birth, The Baby's First Year, The Child from One to Three, The Child from Four to Six.

Contemporary Living
• Teach students how to live independently.
• Discuss eating for good health, budgeting, banking, credit, insurance, housing, managing work and home.

Sociology of the Family
• Students learn how to understand themselves and families better.
• Discuss Individual Development, Communication, Media Influences, Dating, Sexuality, and Adulthood.

HAYLEY ANNE JEREMY
443 Drake Avenue
Ft. Collins, CO 80525
(303) 225-4430

Objective: Family Studies Teacher

EDUCATION
BA, Sociology/Psychology, 1979
Colorado State University, Ft. Collins, CO

Teacher's Certification Program, 1974
University of Northern Colorado, Greeley, CO

CREDENTIALS
Colorado Secondary, Psychology/Sociology, 1974
Colorado Secondary, Elementary Education, 1974

PROFESSIONAL EXPERIENCE

FAMILY STUDIES TEACHER   1974-present
Webber Junior High School, Poudre R-1 School District, Ft. Collins, CO
• Teach Consumer and Family Studies to students Grades 7-9.

Introduction to Consumer and Family Studies
• Teach students activities that help them in everyday living. Topics include:
  - Getting Along with Others, Learning to Be a Wise Consumer, Making Healthy
    Food Choices, Managing Resources, Providing a Living Environment.

Teen Living
• Give students practical experience while exploring the following topics:
  - Present Your Best Self, Feel Great about Yourself, Be a Helpful Family Member,
    Make Good Decisions, Make and Keep Friends, Choosing Your Clothes, Plan and
    Prepare Healthy Meals, and Be a Part of Your School and Community.

Teen Challenges and Choices
• Teach students the thinking skills necessary to cope with a variety of current and
  future decisions on the following issues:
  - Coping with Teen Issues, Managing Time, Money, and Energy, Planning for
    a Job/Career, Teens and the Law, Using Technology at Home, Choosing
    Foods for a Healthy Body, Clothing Options (buy, recycle, sew).
• Provide students with an excellent foundation for planning their high school years.

LOLITA GONZOLAS
2400 Remington Street
Ft. Collins, CO 80524
(303) 224-2109

Objective: Foreign Language Teacher

EDUCATION
BA, Foreign Language, 1979
Colorado State University, Ft. Collins, CO

Teacher's Certification Program, 1974
University of Northern Colorado, Greeley, CO

CREDENTIALS
Colorado Secondary, Foreign Language, Spanish, 1974
Colorado Secondary, Elementary Education, 1974

PROFESSIONAL EXPERIENCE
FOREIGN LANGUAGE TEACHER   1974-present
Ft. Collins High School, Poudre R-1 School District, Ft. Collins, CO
• Teach courses in the Spanish language to students, Grades 10-12.

Spanish I
• Teach students basic conversational Spanish with emphasis on speaking, listening, reading, and writing.
• Introduce students to another culture through videos, games, short readings, and cultural discussions.

Spanish II
• Teach students how to further develop speaking, understanding, reading, and writing of Spanish.
• Students learn about the Spanish people—their customs and lifestyles.
• Accomplish these goals through conversation activities in role playing; reading short stories, magazines, and newspapers; TV productions; games, songs, and language activities.

Spanish III
• Teach students grammar and how to improve the basic skills of listening and speaking, reading, and writing in Spanish.
• Students learn travel vocabulary through short reading selections, listening, comprehension exercises, discussion, and free conversation in groups.
• Study family structure, customs, folklore, music and art, cooking, free-time activities, cities and countries where Spanish language is spoken.

CHARLES E. HASS
125 Smith Street
Ft. Collins, CO 80524
(303) 224-3459

Objective: Foreign Language Teacher

EDUCATION
BA, Foreign Language, 1979
Colorado State University, Ft. Collins, CO

Teacher's Certification Program, 1974
University of Northern Colorado, Greeley, CO

CREDENTIALS
Colorado Secondary, Foreign Language, German, 1974
Colorado Secondary, Elementary Education, 1974

PROFESSIONAL EXPERIENCE
FOREIGN LANGUAGE TEACHER   1974-present
Ft. Collins High School, Poudre R-1 School District, Ft. Collins, CO
- Teach courses in the German language to students, Grades 10-12.

German I
- Teach students basic conversational German with emphasis on speaking, listening, reading, and writing.
- Introduce students to another culture through, videos, games, short readings, and cultural discussions.

German II
- Teach students how to further develop speaking, understanding, reading, and writing of German.
- Students learn about the German people—their customs and lifestyles.
- Accomplish these goals through conversation activities in role playing; reading short stories, magazines, and newspapers; TV productions; games, songs, and language activities.

German III
- Teach students grammar and how to improve the basic skills of listening and speaking, reading, and writing in German.
- Students learn travel vocabulary through short reading selections, listening, comprehension exercises, discussion, and free conversation in groups.
- Study family structure, customs, folklore, music and art, cooking, free-time activities, cities and countries where German language is spoken.

BRUCE STEVEN GUSTIN
332 Terry Shores Drive
Ft. Collins, CO 80524
(303) 224-2210

Objective: Foreign Language Teacher

EDUCATION
BA, Foreign Language, 1979
Colorado State University, Ft. Collins, CO

Teacher's Certification Program, 1974
University of Northern Colorado, Greeley, CO

CREDENTIALS
Colorado Secondary, Foreign Language, French, Latin, 1974
Colorado Secondary, Elementary Education, 1974

PROFESSIONAL EXPERIENCE
FOREIGN LANGUAGE TEACHER   1974-present
Rocky Mountain High School, Poudre R-1 School District, Ft. Collins, CO
- Teach Latin and French language courses to students, Grades 10-12.

Latin I and II
- Teach students Latin vocabulary, grammar, composition, and translation.
- Students learn Latin phrases, abbreviations, and proverbs used in English, along with Roman customs, history, and civilization.
- Students learn to translate stories of Roman culture including the Argonaut Expedition, Caesar's Gallic wars, and history written by other Latin authors.

French IV and V
- Teach students how to further develop conversational skills, reading, and writing of the French language.
- Students explore culture and society demonstrating the differences and similarities between the United States and France.
- Students select literature readings that give insight into the people's thoughts, attitudes, aspirations, lifestyles, and values.
- Students learn from contemporary and past literary works to study techniques and themes and their evolution and significance in the world today.
- Offer students the opportunity to work with native speakers and to visit university language classes.

CLAUDIA A. RENAULT
223 County Road North
Ft. Collins, CO 80521
(303) 224-1129

Objective: Foreign Language Teacher

EDUCATION
BA, Foreign Language, 1979
Colorado State University, Ft. Collins, CO

Teacher's Certification Program, 1974
University of Northern Colorado, Greeley, CO

CREDENTIALS
Colorado Secondary, Foreign Language, French, German, 1974
Colorado Secondary, Elementary Education, 1974

PROFESSIONAL EXPERIENCE
FOREIGN LANGUAGE TEACHER 1974-present
Ft. Collins High School, Poudre R-1 School District, Ft. Collins, CO
- Teach courses in the French language to students, Grades 10-12.

French I
- Teach students basic conversational French with emphasis on speaking, listening, reading, and writing.
- Introduce students to another culture through videos, games, short readings, and cultural discussions.

French II
- Teach students how to further develop speaking, understanding, reading, and writing of French.
- Students learn about the French people—their customs and lifestyles.
- Accomplish these goals through conversation activities in role playing; reading short stories, magazines, and newspapers; TV productions; games, songs, and language activities.

French III
- Teach students grammar and how to improve the basic skills of listening and speaking, reading, and writing in French.
- Students learn through short reading selections, travel vocabulary listening comprehension exercises, discussion, and free conversation in groups.
- Study family structure, customs, folklore, music and art, cooking, free-time activities, cities and countries where French language is spoken.

WILLIAM P. FOX
112 Taft Hill Road
Ft. Collins, CO 80521
(303) 223-1059

OBJECTIVE
Foreign Language Teacher

EDUCATION
BS, Foreign Language, 1979
Colorado State University, Ft. Collins, CO

Teacher's Certification Program, 1974
University of Northern Colorado, Greeley, CO

CREDENTIALS
Colorado Secondary, French, German, Spanish, 1974
Colorado Secondary, Elementary Education, 1974

PROFESSIONAL EXPERIENCE

FOREIGN LANGUAGE TEACHER   1974-present
Lincoln Junior High School, Poudre R-1 School District, Ft. Collins, CO
• Teach French, Spanish, and German language courses to students, Grades 7-9.

Foreign Language Exploration
• Introduce students to the alphabet, numbers, pronunciation, basic phrases, greetings, and culture of Spanish, French, and German languages and their peoples.

Spanish, French, and German 1, 2
• Teach students the skills of listening, speaking, reading, and writing French.
• Educate students on the country and culture of the people.
• Emphasis is placed on the listening and speaking skills with class activities in conversations, dialogues, reading short selections, and written exercises.
• Continued emphasis is on the oral proficiency along with grammar and verbs in Level 2.
  - Continued to teach students about the areas of the world and the United States where the language is spoken.

PREVIOUS EMPLOYMENT HISTORY
Spanish Teacher, Wellington, Junior High, Wellington, CO   1976-79
French Teacher, Lesher Junior High, Ft. Collins, CO   1974-76

BRUCE IAN STEVENSON
3321 Overland Trail
Ft. Collins, CO 80521
(303) 223-4320

OBJECTIVE
History Teacher

EDUCATION
BS, History, 1979
Colorado State University, Ft. Collins, CO

Teacher's Certification Program, 1974
University of Northern Colorado, Greeley, CO

CREDENTIALS
Colorado Secondary, History, 1978
Colorado Secondary, Elementary Education, 1979

PROFESSIONAL EXPERIENCE

HISTORY TEACHER   1985-present
Rocky Mountain High School, Poudre R-1 School District, Ft. Collins, CO
- Teach daily courses in U.S. History and Recent U.S. History to Grades 10-12 in the regular and alternative high school programs.

- Combined field trips, multimedia equipment, student presentations and guest speakers that increased student skills while creating interest and participation.

- Developed a variety of evaluation techniques that improved student performance. Grades 10-12.

TEACHER   1980-85
Centennial High School, Poudre R-1 School District, Ft. Collins, CO
- Taught Social Studies, English, and P.E. with students who could not function in their regular junior high school or Special Education program.

- Developed and implemented an individualized curriculum in Math, Social Studies, and English that improved self-concept, skill level, and performance, Grades 7-10.

PREVIOUS EMPLOYMENT HISTORY
History Teacher, Poudre R-1 School District, Ft. Collins, CO   Summer 1980
Teacher (Alternative Jr. High), Poudre R-1 School District, Ft. Collins, CO   1978-80

CHARLES S. BROWNING
113 Taft Hill Road
Ft. Collins, CO 80521
(303) 224-1559

OBJECTIVE
Industrial Arts Teacher

EDUCATION
MS, Industrial Arts, 1974
University of Northern Colorado, Greeley, CO

BS, Industrial Arts, 1970
University of Northern Colorado, Greeley, CO

SPECIAL CREDENTIALS
Colorado Teaching Credential, Industrial Arts, Life

COMMUNITY SERVICE
Volunteer, RSVP, Ft. Collins, CO, 1992

PROFESSIONAL EXPERIENCE
INDUSTRIAL ARTS TEACHER   1974-present
Ft. Collins High School, Ft. Collins, CO

- Teach students basic industrial arts techniques and assist in development of manipulative skills and shop math.

- Prepare lesson plans for courses and establish goals.

- Lecture, illustrate, and demonstrate when teaching use of handtools including safety practices using lathe, planer, power saws, and drill press.

- Teach students about precision measuring instruments, such as micrometers and industrial arts techniques.

- Evaluate student progress.

- Talk with parents and counselor to resolve behavioral and academic problems.

- Specialize in teaching woodworking and metalworking.

- Teach students with disabilities.

ROBERT C. BAUM
2500 Terry Shores Drive
Ft. Collins, CO 80524
(303) 224-1109

Objective: Journalism Teacher

EDUCATION
BA, Journalism, 1979
Colorado State University, Ft. Collins, CO

Teacher's Certification Program, 1974
University of Northern Colorado, Greeley, CO

CREDENTIALS
Colorado Secondary, Language Arts, Journalism, 1974
Colorado Secondary, Elementary Education, 1974

PROFESSIONAL EXPERIENCE
JOURNALISM TEACHER   1974-present
Rocky Mountain High School, Poudre R-1 School District, Ft. Collins, CO
• Teach Journalism I and II to students, Grades 10-12.

Journalism I
• Teach students how to critically examine professional news reporting and how to write for a newspaper.
• Students learn the fundamentals of news gathering and reporting, interviewing techniques, the essentials of news writing, basic principles of graphic design, and a brief introduction to the layout mechanics of newspaper production.
• Students conduct research and interviewing sources and write several news stories, feature articles, and editorials, imitating the clear, simple, and straightforward style of the journalist.
• Students read the text, participate in class discussions, read the newspaper regularly, keep a "daybook," and take several quizzes and two major exams.

Journalism II
• Students learn on the job and are responsible for production of school newspaper.
• Students perform as editor, reporter, business manager, photographer, ad sales person, or artist, depending on their position on the newspaper staff.
• Students learn how to be an exceptionally hardworking team, making decisions, and meeting strict deadline schedules while turning in quality work.

GEORGE C. CAMERON
3021 Terry Shores Drive
Ft. Collins, CO 80524
(303) 224-7789

Objective: Journalism Teacher

EDUCATION
BA, Journalism, 1979
Colorado State University, Ft. Collins, CO

Teacher's Certification Program, 1974
University of Northern Colorado, Greeley, CO

CREDENTIALS
Colorado Secondary, Language Arts, Journalism, 1974
Colorado Secondary, Elementary Education, 1974

PROFESSIONAL EXPERIENCE

JOURNALISM TEACHER   1974-present
Ft. Collins High School, Poudre R-1 School District, Ft. Collins, CO
• Teach Writing for Literary Publications courses to students, Grades 10-12.

Writing for Literary Publications
• Teach students to focus on qualities of good writing and editing skills.
• Students read literary publications and look for illustrations of good writing style.
• Students study and practice editing skills for accuracy, conciseness, and clarity.
• Students participate in writing workshops for their own writing and reviewing others' writing.
• Students serve as publication editors by commenting on and returning submissions for revisions by writer or by editing works for publication.
• Students review submissions while serving on the editorial board.
• Students learn how to design and prepare publications for student writing representing a variety of writing from various classes at Ft. Collins High School and publish the *Looking Glass*, the annual literary publication.
• Students experience reviewing and choosing works for publication, editing, designing layout, printing, and distributing publications.
• Students also write for school publications including yearbook, literary magazine, and parent newsletter.

HOLLY K. JONES
1904 Scarlet Oak Drive
Oakdale, CA 95361
(209) 847-0032

OBJECTIVE
Elementary-School Teacher

EDUCATION
Multiple Subject Teaching Credential, 1991
California State University, Stanislaus, CA, GPA: 3.86

BA, Sociology, 1989
University of California, Santa Barbara, CA

PROFESSIONAL PROFILE
- Team player with teachers, administrator and parents.
- Highly organized, dedicated with a positive attitude.
- Communicate effectively with all types of people.
- Work well in a competitive and challenging environment.
- Strength in assessing people's needs while gaining trust and confidence.
- Skilled problem solver with proven leadership qualities.

TEACHING EXPERIENCE

EL PORTAL, Escalon School District   Spring 1991
Student Teacher (Grade 6)
- Recognize the needs of students and promote the total growth of each child involving social, emotional, intellectual, creative, and physical behavior.

CHRYSLER SCHOOL, Stanislaus Union School District
Student Teacher (Grade 3)   Spring 1991
- Develop lesson plans and teach all areas of the curriculum to a multicultural classroom of bilingual, low-achieving, and gifted students.
- Introduced a science unit on water conservation as part of a project for the annual science fair.
    - Project involved cooperative learning groups and hands-on experiences.
- Maintain positive classroom discipline on a daily basis.
- Participate in parent/teacher conferences.
- Help low-achieving students with after-school homework and activities.

- More -

TEACHING EXPERIENCE (Continued)

MAGNOLIA ELEMENTARY SCHOOL, Oakdale School District   Winter 1991
Chapter 1 Teacher (Grade 4-6)
- Analyzed student test scores to determine and to help with areas of weakness.
  - Developed instructions to meet those needs.
- Conferenced with teachers on each student's progress.
- Developed and implemented instructional material for math and language arts.

STANISLAUS COUNTY (Department of Education)
Substitute Teacher (K-6)
- Worked with five school districts throughout the county.
- Implemented lessons and plans while maintaining positive classroom discipline in the teacher's absence.

AFFILIATIONS
Member, American Teachers Association

LOCATION OF PLACEMENT PAPERS
Educational Careers
Counseling and Career Services
University of California at Santa Barbara
Santa Barbara, CA 93106
(805) 961-4416

NANCY R. KELLY
553 Palm Avenue
Carpinteria, CA 93013
(805) 684-2123

OBJECTIVE
Elementary-School Teacher

EDUCATION
Multiple Subject Teaching Credential, 1987
University of California, Santa Barbara, CA, GPA: 4.0

BA, Religious Studies, 1986
University of California, Santa Barbara, CA

SPECIAL TRAINING
Received special training in the following student-oriented teaching techniques: Mastery learning, Team Teaching—Peer Coaching, Cooperative Learning, Writing across the Curriculum, Using Computers in the Classroom, Bloom's Taxonomy, Behavior Modification and Management, Differential Instruction, ESL, Project Aims Mathematics and Science, Project Wild, Math-Their-Way, DRTA, Read Aloud, Reader's Theatre, Language Experience Approach (LEA), Reading Assessment Diagnosis Using IRI Cloze and Miscue Analysis, Teaching Science through Guided Discovery.

STUDENT TEACHING EXPERIENCE

STUDENT TEACHER (Grades 2-3)   1987-present
Montecito Union School, Montecito, CA
- Teach all areas of curriculum to classes of 30 students.
- Instruct classes using the team teaching concept, curriculum specialists, classroom aides, parent volunteers, and preprofessionals in the classroom.

STUDENT TEACHER (Grade 6)   1986-87
Summerland School, Summerland, CA
- Instructed all areas of curriculum to 30 students in a small rural environment.
- Planned and taught language arts, HBJ Math and processed student progress evaluations.
- Attended Parent/Teacher/Student Conferences.

- More -

PROFESSIONAL EXPERIENCE

INSTRUCTIONAL AIDE (Kindergarten, Bilingual)   Summers 1984-86
Canalino School, (Early Childhood Learning Center), Carpinteria, CA
- Worked with a variety of groups of children helping them to develop basic skills.
- Taught cognitive skills including numbers, letter recognition and sequencing, and arts and crafts under the supervision of the teacher.
- Served as After-School Reading Program Director.
  - Developed, administered, and taught a specialized program created especially for students needing improvement with their reading abilities.
  - Tutored students one-on-one who needed improvement with their reading.
  - Organized and coordinated classroom materials for students in the library.

INSTRUCTIONAL AIDE (Grades 1-6)   Summers 1984-86
Summerland School, Summerland, CA
- Prepared materials for classroom use and student progress evaluation.
- Taught children Reading, Math, and Art.
- Assisted teacher with playground supervision for as many as 60 students.

AFFILIATIONS
Member, American Teachers Association

LOCATION OF PLACEMENT PAPERS
Educational Careers
Counseling and Career Services
University of California at Santa Barbara
Santa Barbara, CA 93106
(805) 961-4416

JONAH C. NICHOLS
320 East Sola Street
Santa Barbara, CA 93101
(805) 963-4409

OBJECTIVE
Elementary-School Teacher

EDUCATION
Multiple Subject Teaching Credential, 1989
California State University, Chico, CA, GPA: 4.0

BS, Education, 1989
Brigham Young University, Provo, UT

TEACHING EXPERIENCE
TEACHER (Grades K-2)   1990-present
Richmond School District, Susanville, CA
• Instruct multicultural classroom environment in an urban area.
• Teach all areas of curriculum to 30 students with strong emphasis on developing phonics program, creative writing, math, and science.

TEACHER (Grades 6-7)   1989-90
Granite School District, Salt Lake City, UT
• Instructed all areas of curriculum to 30 students in a small rural environment.
• Coached the cross-country and basketball teams.
• Led the environmental camp.
• Served on the Science Fair Board of Directors, academic olympic committees, site council, fund-raising events, and mentor teacher program, and supervised student teachers.

PROFESSIONAL PROFILE
• Strong interpersonal communication skills with cross-cultural sensitivity.
• Highly organized, dedicated with a positive attitude.
• Communicate effectively with all types of people.
• Work well in a competitive, growth environment.
• Strength in assessing student needs while gaining trust and confidence.
• Skilled problem solver with proven leadership qualities.

- More -

AFFILIATIONS
Member, American Teachers Association

LOCATION OF PLACEMENT PAPERS
Educational Careers
Counseling and Career Services
Brigham Young University
Provo, UT 84602
(801) 378-4416

CAROLINE SUZANNA GANITE
993 Windmill Drive
Lake Elsinore, CA 92330
(714) 244-8032

OBJECTIVE
Elementary-School Teacher

EDUCATION
Multiple Subject Teaching Credential, 1987
University of California, Santa Barbara, CA, GPA: 4.0

BA, Business Administration, 1986
University of California at Santa Barbara

SPECIAL TRAINING
Received special training in the following student-oriented teaching techniques: Mastery learning, Team Teaching—Peer Coaching, Cooperative Learning, Writing across the Curriculum, Using Computers in the Classroom, Bloom's Taxonomy, Behavior Modification and Management, Differential Instruction, ESL, Project Aims Mathematics and Science, Project Wild, Math-Their-Way, DRTA, Read Aloud, Reader's Theatre, Language Experience Approach (LEA), Reading Assessment Diagnosis Using IRI Cloze and Miscue Analysis, Teaching Science through Guided Discovery.

CLASSROOM EXPERIENCE

TEACHER (Grade 6)   1988-present
Railroad Canyon School, Lake Elsinore, CA
- Invited to teach all areas of curriculum to classes of 30 students at this new school of 1300 multicultural students.
- Work closely with a visually disabled and limited English proficiency student.
- Instruct classes using the team teaching concept, curriculum specialists, classroom aides, parent volunteers, and preprofessionals in the classroom.
- Initiated sixth grade peer tutoring service for students with lower grades.
- Serve as Student Council Advisor, Social Studies Curriculum Committee Member.
- Secured Community Sponsors for School, and District Discipline Planning Board.
- Certified for ELPS training.

- More -

CLASSROOM EXPERIENCE (Continued)

TEACHER (Grade 6)   **1987-88**
<u>Butterfield Elementary School</u>, Lake Elsinore, CA
- Instructed all areas of curriculum to 30 students as well as the Accelerated Above Grade Level Reading class in a multicultural classroom setting.
- Served on the Home-Teaching Planning and Writing and Self-Esteem Committees.
- Attend numerous professional growth seminars.
- Served as peer coach for the volleyball, basketball, and intramural sports.
- Functioned as school duel coach for academic competition for entire district.
- Became community sponsor for team uniforms and spelling bee trophies and awards.

AFFILIATIONS
Member, <u>American Teachers Association</u>

LOCATION OF PLACEMENT PAPERS
Educational Careers
Counseling and Career Services
University of California at Santa Barbara
Santa Barbara, CA 93106
(805) 961-4416

DIANNE PAULINA FASTONE
334 Broderick Way
Port Hueneme, CA 93041
(805) 984-7223

OBJECTIVE
Elementary-School Teacher

EDUCATION
Multiple Subject Teaching Credential, 1987
University of California, Santa Barbara, CA, GPA: 4.0

BA, English, 1986
University of California at Santa Barbara

SPECIAL TRAINING
Received special training in the following student-oriented teaching techniques: Mastery learning, Team Teaching — Peer Coaching, Cooperative Learning, Writing across the Curriculum, Using Computers in the Classroom, Bloom's Taxonomy, Behavior Modification and Management, Differential Instruction, ESL, Project Aims Mathematics and Science, Project Wild, Math-Their-Way, DRTA, Read Aloud, Reader's Theatre, Language Experience Approach (LEA), Reading Assessment Diagnosis Using IRI Cloze and Miscue Analysis, Teaching Science through Guided Discovery.

CLASSROOM EXPERIENCE

STUDENT TEACHER (Grade 1)   1987-present
Montecito Union School, Montecito, CA
- Teach all areas of curriculum to classes of 30 students.
- Instruct classes using the team teaching concept, curriculum specialists, classroom aides, parent volunteers, and preprofessionals in the classroom.

STUDENT TEACHER (Grades 4-6)   1986-87
Summerland School, Summerland, CA
- Instructed all areas of curriculum to 30 students in a small rural environment.
- Planned and taught language arts, reading, creative writing, physical education, mathematics, and literature in this two-room schoolhouse.

- More -

AFFILIATIONS
Member, American Teachers Association

LOCATION OF PLACEMENT PAPERS
Educational Careers
Counseling and Career Services
University of California at Santa Barbara
Santa Barbara, CA 93106
(805) 961-4416

MOLLY P. BLAKELY

	Permanent Address
I I I Camanno # I	2215 Oak Street
Goleta, CA 93117	San Francisco, CA 94361
(805) 362-8899	(415) 888-1177

Objective: Grades K-6 Teaching position

PROFESSIONAL PROFILE
- Team player with teachers, administrators, and parents.
- Work well in a competitive and challenging environment.
- Skilled problem solver with proven leadership qualities.

EDUCATION
- California Basic Educational Skills Test (CBEST) Passed in April 1989.

- **BA Degree, Sociology**, June 1990
  University of California, Los Angeles

CLASSROOM EXPERIENCE

1988-90 **PREPROFESSIONAL VOLUNTEER INSTRUCTOR**
El Camino Elementary School, Los Angeles School District
- Assisted teacher of 3rd grade students with daily classroom activities in all areas of the curriculum.
  - Worked with groups as well as on a one-on-one basis.
- Concerned with the total growth and needs of the child involving social, emotional, intellectual, creative, and physical behavior.
- Built child's self-esteem and self confidence. Effectively motivated children to maximize participation and enjoyment.
- Supervised children on field trips.

Fall 1987 **PREPROFESSIONAL VOLUNTEER INSTRUCTOR**
Blakely School, Los Angeles School District
- Assisted the teacher with instruction of kindergarten children.
  - Worked with children on a one-on-one basis and in small groups in this classroom of 20 students.
- Identified and provided assistance to children needing special attention with above or below average skills.
  - Promoted behavior based on respect for others, teaching children to communicate their feelings and to hear each other.
  - Provided consistent behavior/progress, each child at his or her own pace.
  - Focused on respect for child's strengths and unique personality.
- Supervised art projects, and math games and worked with children on manipulative math activities and reading readiness.

GERTI J. KOWKOSKI
490 Wilcox Lane
Ft. Collins, CO 80524
(303) 224-1100

OBJECTIVE
Language Arts Teacher

EDUCATION
BA, Journalism, 1979
Colorado State University, Ft. Collins, CO

Teacher's Certification Program, 1974
University of Northern Colorado, Greeley, CO

CREDENTIALS
Colorado Secondary, Language Arts, Journalism, 1974
Colorado Secondary, Elementary Education, 1974

PROFESSIONAL EXPERIENCE

LANGUAGE ARTS, JOURNALISM TEACHER   1974-present
Lesher Junior High School, Poudre R-1 School District, Ft. Collins, CO
• Teach Journalism courses to interested and capable writer students, Grades 8-9.

Journalism/Newspaper 8/9
• Introduce students to the basic skills involved in the publication of a newspaper.
• Teach students journalistic style, editing, interviewing, layout and design, and the responsibility of the press.
• Emphasize news writing and meeting deadlines.

Yearbook 8/9
• Teach students all phases of yearbook production.
• Students learn to design layouts, write copy, organize materials, select photographs, and function as a cooperative member of a publication staff.

PREVIOUS EMPLOYMENT HISTORY
Language Arts Teacher, Poudre R-1 School District, Ft. Collins, CO   1974-79
Freelance Writer, The Coloradoan, Ft. Collins, CO   1972-present

DAPHNEY R. LIPPMAN
126 Lake Street
Ft. Collins, CO 80524
(303) 224-3300

Objective: Drama Teacher

EDUCATION
BA, Drama, 1979
Colorado State University, Ft. Collins, CO

Teacher's Certification Program, 1974
University of Northern Colorado, Greeley, CO

CREDENTIALS
Colorado Secondary, **Language Arts, 1974**
Colorado Secondary, **Elementary Education, 1974**

PROFESSIONAL EXPERIENCE
LANGUAGE ARTS TEACHER   1974-present
Boltz Junior High School, Poudre R-1 School District, Ft. Collins, CO
- Teach Drama and Basic Speech courses in the Language Arts Department to students, Grades 8-9.

Drama 1
- Introduce or improve basic acting skills and techniques to develop and practice creative imagination and self-discipline.
  - Teach students character creation and interpretation, improvisation, pantomime, and oral interpretation.
  - Educate students on the study of stagecraft and dramatic literature.
  - Students have the opportunity to perform in front of others.

Drama 2
- Teach students to advance and polish existing acting skills. Character analysis, script interpretation, character creation, and script memorization are focused.
- Students learn play production, selecting a script, casting, tryouts, backstage crews, and performance and theatre etiquette.

Basic Speech
- Teach students to improve public speaking.
- Classes address the organization, preparation, and delivery of solo speaking. This includes informative, visual aid, demonstration, and persuasive speeches.
- Educate students on effective listening, oral interpretation, and group discussion.

KIT R. HOUSTON
111 Mulberry Avenue
Ft. Collins, CO 80521
(303) 224-2219

Objective: Language Arts Teacher

EDUCATION
BA, Language Arts, 1979
Colorado State University, Ft. Collins, CO

Teacher's Certification Program, 1974
University of Northern Colorado, Greeley, CO

CREDENTIALS
Colorado Secondary, Language Arts, Reading, 1974
Colorado Secondary, Elementary Education, 1974

PROFESSIONAL EXPERIENCE

LANGUAGE ARTS TEACHER 1974-present
Cach La Poudre Junior High School, Poudre R-1 School District, Ft. Collins, CO
- Teach Reading courses in the Language Arts Department to students, Grades 8-9.

Reading 8/9
- Teach reading to students who have difficulty with textbook reading assignments.
- Emphasize reinforcement of basic reading, comprehension, vocabulary, and study-reading skills in Reading 8/9.
- Provide students with drills to improve comprehension of literature and technical text, and to develop skills in reading paperback novels; reading for facts, reading to solve reasoning problems; reading to form critical opinions; reading for recreation.

Reading Laboratory
- Teach students how to increase reading and study skills through an intense, self-paced, individualized program.
- Students learn to manage time, set goals, follow directions, take notes, prepare for tests, and improve memory.
- Train Students to use materials and class time effectively, based on pretest of comprehension, vocabulary, study skills, and rate.

Outstanding Authors 8/9
- Provide reading and discussion time for students interested in reading well-known books and short stories by outstanding writers.
- Discussions, patterned after "Great Books" model, emphasize reasoning problems, inference thinking, critical reaction, and opinions as comprehension skills.

STEFEN S. KINGSTON
808 Lorie Park Way
Ft. Collins, CO 80521
(303) 224-3321

OBJECTIVE
Mathematics Teacher

EDUCATION
BS, Mathematics, 1979
Colorado State University, Ft. Collins, CO

Teacher's Certification Program, 1974
University of Northern Colorado, Greeley, CO

CREDENTIALS
Colorado Secondary, Mathematics, 1978
Colorado Secondary, Elementary Education, 1979

PROFESSIONAL EXPERIENCE

MATHEMATICS TEACHER   1978-present
Rocky Mountain High School, Poudre R-1 School District, Ft. Collins, CO
- Teach daily courses in Geometry, Trigonometry, and Calculus to Grades 10-12.
- Combined cooperative learning, problem solving, learning contracts, guest speakers, evaluation techniques, and student reports that increased comprehension, study skills, classroom participation and motivation.

Pre-Calculus and Calculus BC
- Teach students in Pre-Calculus how to solve problems with particular emphasis on trigonometry and analytic geometry.
- Study polynomial, logarithmic and exponential functions as well as vectors, polar coordinates, and limits.
- Teach students Calculus BC limits, derivatives of algebraic functions, applications of the derivatives, applications of the definite integral, transcendental functions, methods of integration, analytic geometry, and polar coordinates.
- Prepare students to take the AP Calculus test.

Geometry
- Teach students an understanding of a mathematical system using the properties of geometry developed through inductive and deductive reasoning.
- Topics taught are angle measure, triangles, circles, polygons, parallel lines, the coordinate plane, areas, and volumes, and elementary techniques of applying algebra to geometry.

BRYCE J. WARREN
228 Cherry Creek Way
Ft. Collins, CO 80521
(303) 224-8967

OBJECTIVE
Mathematics Teacher

EDUCATION
BS, Mathematics, 1979
Colorado State University, Ft. Collins, CO

Teacher's Certification Program, 1974
University of Northern Colorado, Greeley, CO

CREDENTIALS
Colorado Secondary, Mathematics, 1978
Colorado Secondary, Elementary Education, 1979

PROFESSIONAL EXPERIENCE

MATHEMATICS TEACHER   1985-present
Lesher School, Poudre R-1 School District, Ft. Collins, CO
- Teach daily courses in Algebra and Geometry to students, Grades 7-9.
- Combined cooperative learning, problem solving, learning contracts, guest speakers, evaluation techniques, and student reports that increased comprehension, study skills, classroom participation, and motivation.

Algebra 1, 2
- Teach students how to solve problems using variables and mathematical properties with algebraic functions, factoring, and solving systems of equations.
- Emphasize further strengthening of algebraic concepts, manipulation, and development of problem-solving skills in Algebra 2.
- Cover linear equalities and inequalities, absolute value, function, linear systems, factorization techniques, polynomials, binomial expansion, functional notation, radicals, quadratic equations, logarithmic and exponential functions.

Geometry
- Teach students an understanding of a mathematical system through the use of inductive and deductive reasoning.
- Topics taught are angle measure, triangles, circles, polygons, parallel lines, the coordinate plane, areas and volumes, and elementary techniques of applying algebra to geometry.

GARTH B. GUNDERSON
3321 Livermore Drive
Ft. Collins, CO 80521
(303) 224-2212

OBJECTIVE
Mathematics Teacher

EDUCATION
BS, Mathematics, 1979
Colorado State University, Ft. Collins, CO

Teacher's Certification Program, 1974
University of Northern Colorado, Greeley, CO

CREDENTIALS
Colorado Secondary, Mathematics, 1978
Colorado Secondary, Elementary Education, 1979

PROFESSIONAL EXPERIENCE

MATHEMATICS TEACHER   1985-present
Rocky Mountain High School, Poudre R-1 School District, Ft. Collins, CO
- Teach daily courses in Basic Math, Consumer Math, Introduction to Algebra, Algebra 1, and Algebra 2 to students, Grades 10-12.
- Combined cooperative learning, problem solving, learning contracts, guest speakers, evaluation techniques, and student reports that increased comprehension, study skills, classroom participation, and motivation.

TEACHER, TUTOR, COMPUTER RESOURCE AIDE, SUBSTITUTE   1980-85
Centennial High School, Poudre R-1 School District, Ft. Collins, CO
- Taught Introduction to Typing, Keyboarding and Word Processing, Introduction to Micro-Computers and Elective Week classes to Grades 9-12.
- Tutored Math and Reading.
- Substituted in Math, Social Studies, Science, Reading, and English.
- Planned, promoted, and established computer-assisted instruction in Math, Reading, English/Language Arts, Career Education, and Social Studies that improved comprehension and expanded student mastery of computer literacy.

PREVIOUS EMPLOYMENT HISTORY
Mathematics Teacher, Poudre R-1 School District, Ft. Collins, CO   Summer 1980
Teacher (Alternative Jr. High), Poudre R-1 School District, Ft. Collins, CO 1978-80

TRACY L. JUNIPER
2129 Lake Street
Ft. Collins, CO 80524
(303) 224-2227

OBJECTIVE
Mentally Impaired Teacher position

EDUCATION
MA, Special Education, 1974
University of Northern Colorado, Greeley

BA, Special Education, 1970
University of California, Santa Barbara, CA

SPECIAL CREDENTIALS
Learning Handicapped Specialist Teaching Credential, Life
Multiple Subject Teaching Credential, K-12, Life
Certified by the county, state and federal government

PROFESSIONAL EXPERIENCE
TEACHER, MENTALLY IMPAIRED   1974-present
Poudre R-1 School District, Ft. Collins, CO
- Teach elementary and secondary school subjects and living skills to students with mental impairments in the Poudre R-1 School District.
- Plan curriculum and prepare lessons according to achievement levels to meet individual needs of students.
- Confer with parents, administrators, testing specialists, social workers, and others to develop individualized educational programs for students.
- Instruct students in academic subjects, utilizing phonetics, multisensory learning, and repetition to reinforce learning.
- Instruct students in daily living skills required for independent maintenance and economic self-sufficiency, such as hygiene, safety, and food preparation.
- Observe, evaluate, and prepare reports on progress of students.
- Meet with parents to provide support and guidance in using community resources.

PROFESSIONAL AFFILIATIONS
Council on Exceptional Children - Mental Retardation Division

PREVIOUS EMPLOYMENT HISTORY
Teacher, Mentally Impaired, Goleta Valley School District, Goleta, CA   1970-74

CYNTHIA R. CAROLYN
395 Yorkshire Drive
Santa Barbara, CA 93103
(805) 683-2381

Objective: Montessori teacher position

EDUCATION
Montessori Method of Education
St Nicholas Training Centre, Diploma, 1980

PROFESSIONAL PROFILE
- Team player with assistants, administrators, and parents.
- Skilled problem solver. Promote harmonious relationships.
- Received teacher certificates for every major workshop and convention held in Santa Barbara in the past 10 years.
- Classroom was filmed on a video used in a television news special highlighting my teaching skills and expertise.

PROFESSIONAL EXPERIENCE
Teacher, Montessori School of Santa Barbara   1980-present

Classroom Teaching
- Teach all areas of the curriculum to groups of 25 children ages 2-6. Subjects include science, geography, writing, English and Spanish language, and sensory exploration.
  - Implement structure and freedom to provide a balance through developmentally appropriate activities.
  - Coordinate special materials and guest speakers for unique classroom lessons.

Effective Teaching Methods
- Concerned with the total growth and needs of the child involving social, emotional, intellectual, creative, and physical behavior.
  - Promote behavior based on respect for others, teaching children to communicate their feelings and to hear each other.
  - Provide consistent behavior and progress each child at his/her own pace. Respect each child's strengths and unique personality.

Quotes From Parents
- "Cynthia has the ability to make each child feel unique and special. She has been a mainstay in our children's education and has truly made a difference in their lives." Ruth Roscoe, Principal, parent of two children, June, 1986.

- "Our daughters, Annie and Elizabeth have blossomed with Cynthia. She has shown those little girls how exciting learning can be. What a wonderful gift Cynthia has with children. Annie and Elizabeth will never forget her." Margaret Shannon, Administrator, 1991

JOHN S. DAVIDSON
114 Riverview Road
Ft. Collins, CO 80524
(303) 223-3909

Objective: Music Teacher

EDUCATION
BA, Music, 1979
Colorado State University, Ft. Collins, CO

Teacher's Certification Program, 1974
University of Northern Colorado, Greeley, CO

CREDENTIALS
Colorado Secondary, **Music**, 1974
Colorado Secondary, **Elementary Education**, 1974

PROFESSIONAL EXPERIENCE
MUSIC TEACHER   1974-present
Ft. Collins High School, Poudre R-1 School District, Ft. Collins, CO
• Teach Band and Orchestra to students, Grades 10-12.

Rocky Mountain Winds
• Teach basic skills to beginning wind, brass, and percussion players.
• Emphasize tone, technical facility, music terminology, and music reading.
• Present appropriate literature and performance opportunities.
• Intermediate band emphasizes fundamentals such as scales, chords, and tone production with a large quantity of band literature of varying styles and difficulty.
• Students in advanced band will participate in symphony orchestra twice a week.
• Students develop advanced playing techniques through required rehearsals and performances.

Symphony Orchestra
• Teach students basic techniques of bowing, fingering, and correct manipulation of string instruments.
• Present appropriate literature to students and performance opportunities.
• Instruct students in advanced orchestra music ranging from Early Baroque through contemporary and popular styles.
• Students are required to perform both as a string ensemble and as a symphony orchestra by combining woodwinds, brass, and percussion.

WILLIAM S. STEVENS
227 Riverside Drive
Ft. Collins, CO 80524
(303) 223-2200

Objective: Music Teacher

EDUCATION
BA, Music, 1979
Colorado State University, Ft. Collins, CO

Teacher's Certification Program, 1974
University of Northern Colorado, Greeley, CO

CREDENTIALS
Colorado Secondary, Music, 1974
Colorado Secondary, Elementary Education, 1974

PROFESSIONAL EXPERIENCE

MUSIC TEACHER   1974-present
Blevens Junior High School, Poudre R-1 School District, Ft. Collins, CO
• Teach Band and Orchestra to students, Grades 7-9.

Junior High Band
• Teach basic skills to beginning wind, brass, and percussion players.
• Emphasize tone, technical facility, music terminology, and music reading.
• Present appropriate literature and performance opportunities.
• Intermediate band emphasizes fundamentals such as scales, chords, and tone production with a large quantity of band literature of varying styles and difficulty.
• Students in advanced band will participate in symphony orchestra twice a week.
• Students develop advanced playing techniques through required rehearsals and performances.

Junior High Orchestra
• Teach students basic techniques of bowing, fingering, and correct manipulation of string instruments.
• Present appropriate literature to students and performance opportunities.
• Instruct students in advanced orchestra the study of music ranging from Early Baroque through contemporary and popular styles.
• Students are required to perform both as a string ensemble and as a symphony orchestra by combining woodwinds, brass, and percussion.

PREVIOUS EMPLOYMENT HISTORY
Music Teacher, Poudre R-1 School District, Ft. Collins, CO   1974-79

RACHEL S. WALTNER
11 Smith Street
Ft. Collins, CO 80524
(303) 224-2419

Objective: Music Teacher

EDUCATION
BA, Music, 1979
Colorado State University, Ft. Collins, CO

Teacher's Certification Program, 1974
University of Northern Colorado, Greeley, CO

CREDENTIALS
Colorado Secondary, Music, 1974
Colorado Secondary, Elementary Education, 1974

PROFESSIONAL EXPERIENCE
MUSIC TEACHER   1974-present
Lincoln Junior High School, Poudre R-1 School District, Ft. Collins, CO
- Teach Choir Courses in the Music Department to students, Grades 7-9.

Choir Grades 7, 8, 9
- Explore different musical styles and development of skills that are basic to musical understanding and appreciation and instruction in vocal techniques in Choir 7.
  - Teach students preparation, knowledge, and skills that build confidence in adolescent singers by performing in class.
  - Prepare students for advanced choirs in eighth and ninth grade.
- Give gifted and talented students opportunity to perform concerts in the school and community in Choir 8 and 9.

Women's Choir Grades 8, 9
- Teach choir to soprano and alto voices and perform music of intermediate difficulty, which prepares students for further advanced study in music.
- Students perform at school and in the community.

Guitar
- Train students in fundamental theory in reading and playing notes, rhythms, chords, scales, and accompaniment styles in guitar.

PREVIOUS EMPLOYMENT HISTORY
Music Teacher, Poudre R-1 School District, Ft. Collins, CO   1974-79

RONNA SUE YOKOM
115 Sheeley Street
Ft. Collins, CO 80524
(303) 224-1987

OBJECTIVE
Physical Education Teacher

EDUCATION
MS, Physical Education, 1974
University of Northern Colorado, Greeley

BS, Special Education, 1970
University of Northern Colorado, Greeley, CO

SPECIAL CREDENTIALS
Adapted Physical Education Credential, Life
Colorado Multiple Subject Teaching Credential, K-12, Life

PROFESSIONAL EXPERIENCE

TEACHER, PHYSICAL EDUCATION   1974-present
Rocky Mountain High School, Ft. Collins, CO
- Plan physical education programs to promote development of student's physical attributes and social skills.
- Teach individual and team sports to students, utilizing knowledge of sports techniques and of physical capabilities of students.
- Organize, lead, instruct, and referee indoor and outdoor games, such as volleyball, baseball, and basketball.
- Instruct individuals and groups in beginning and advanced calisthenics, gymnastics, and corrective exercises.
- Determine type and level of difficulty of exercises needed and prescribe movements, applying knowledge of sports, physiology, and corrective techniques.
- Teach and demonstrate use of gymnastic and training apparatus, such as trampolines and weights.
- Confer with students, parents, and school counselor to resolve student problems.
- Select, store, order, issue, and inventory equipment, materials, and supplies used in physical education program.
- Teach students with disabilities.

PREVIOUS EMPLOYMENT HISTORY
Physical Education Teacher, Blevins Junior High, Ft. Collins, CO   **1970-74**

SAMUEL DEAN ALTMAN
210 Smith Street
Ft. Collins, CO 80524
(303) 224-9039

Objective: Physical Education Teacher

EDUCATION
BA, Physical Education, 1979
Colorado State University, Ft. Collins, CO

Teacher's Certification Program, 1974
University of Northern Colorado, Greeley, CO

CREDENTIALS
Colorado Secondary, **Physical Education, 1974**
Colorado Secondary, **Elementary Education, 1974**

PROFESSIONAL EXPERIENCE
PHYSICAL EDUCATION TEACHER   1974-present
Blevins Junior High School, Poudre R-1 School District, Ft. Collins, CO
• Teach Physical Education to students, Grades 7-9.

Physical Education 7, 8, 9
• Help students to develop physical fitness and wellness, desirable social traits, knowledge of a variety of activities and motor skills.

• Teach students soccer, volleyball, flag football, basketball, softball, tumbling, and racquet skills.

• Educate students with aerobics, fitness testing, track and field, and rhythms.

• Schedule a Scoliosis screening by the school nurse and physical education staff.

Positive Physical Education
• Introduce physical activities that educate and match average motor-skilled students with students needing help in a one-on-one situation to offer improvement on motor skills, self-esteem, and self-concept.

PREVIOUS EMPLOYMENT HISTORY
Physical Education Teacher, Poudre R-1 School District, Ft. Collins, CO   1974-79

KATE S. RYAN
1450 McConnel Drive
Ft. Collins, CO 80521
(303) 224-2209

OBJECTIVE
Physically Impaired Teacher position

EDUCATION
MA, Special Education, 1974
University of Northern Colorado, Greeley, CO

BA, Special Education, 1970
University of Northern Colorado, Greeley, CO

SPECIAL CREDENTIALS
Learning Handicapped Specialist Teaching Credential, Life
Multiple Subject Teaching Credential, K-12, Life

PROFESSIONAL EXPERIENCE
TEACHER, PHYSICALLY IMPAIRED   1974-present
Poudre R-1 School District, Ft. Collins, CO
- Teach elementary and secondary school subjects to physically impaired students, adapting methods of instruction to meet individual needs of students in schools, hospitals, and students' homes.
- Plan curriculum and prepare lessons and materials, considering individual needs, abilities, learning levels, and physical limitations of students.
- Confer with parents, administrators, testing specialists, social worker, therapists, and others to develop educational programs for students.
- Instruct students with observable orthopedic impairments as well as those with internal impairment, such as heart condition.
- Arrange and adjust tools, work aids, and equipment utilized by students in classroom, such as equipped worktables, computers, typewriters, and mechanized page turners.
- Devise special teaching tools, techniques, and equipment.
- Instruct students in academic subjects and other activities designed to provide a positive learning experience.
- Confer with staff members to develop programs to maximize students' potentials.
- Assist members of medical staff in rehabilitation programs for students.

PROFESSIONAL AFFILIATIONS
- Association for Children and Adults with Learning Disabilities (ACALD) - Ft. Collins, CO, since 1974

SCOTT WILLIAM EDWARDS

Current Address:
1234 Sabado Tarde #1
Goleta, CA 93117
(805) 966-1234

Permanent Address:
2220 Santa Ana Street
Ventura, CA 93004
(805) 682-0987

OBJECTIVE
Teaching position at a private school, Grades 9-12

EDUCATION
BA, Biochemistry/Molecular Biology
University of California, Santa Barbara, CA
GPA: 3.8   Graduation: June 1990

PROFESSIONAL PROFILE
- Financed education with experience as a teacher and counselor.
- Special talent for motivating people of all backgrounds.
- Work well under pressure situations maintaining a professional and concerned manner.
- Achieved the Dean's Honor List at UCSB 10 times.

RELATED EXPERIENCE

Teaching Skills
- Tutor math, biology, physics, general and organic chemistry to college students on a one-on-one basis as well as in small group sessions.
  - Deal effectively with students of all levels and learning abilities.
  - Strong ability to present subject matter in multiple context tailored to individual needs.
  - Outstanding ability to motivate uninterested individuals in required nonmajor subjects.
- Taught private and public swim lessons to children and adults.
  - Instructed individuals and groups from beginners to competitive levels.

Communication Skills
- Conduct educational presentations to groups of 25-150 elementary, junior, and high school students throughout the Santa Barbara community.
  - Provide awareness concerning relationships with a disabled person in the community.
- Counsel and instruct disabled children and adolescents at the Santa Barbara Junior Wheelchair Sports Camp.
  - Effectively motivate campers to learn new activities including:
    tennis...basketball...swimming...track & field...weight lifting...archery
  - Provide continued support as a role model to handle real-life situations.

EMPLOYMENT HISTORY
Private Tutor, Self Employed, Santa Barbara, CA   1986-present
Instructor/Counselor, Santa Barbara Wheelchair Sports Camp   1987-89

MADELINE S. PARTRIDGE
340 Willox Lane
Ft. Collins, CO 80524
(303) 224-1110

Objective: Social Studies Teacher

EDUCATION
BS, Psychology, 1979
Colorado State University, Ft. Collins, CO

Teacher's Certification Program, 1974
University of Northern Colorado, Greeley, CO

CREDENTIALS
Colorado Secondary, Social Studies, Psychology, 1974
Colorado Secondary, Elementary Education, 1974

PROFESSIONAL EXPERIENCE
SOCIAL STUDIES TEACHER   1974-present
Rocky Mountain High School, Poudre R-1 School District, Ft. Collins, CO
- Teach courses in Psychology and Sociology of the Family through the Social Studies Department to students, Grades 10-12.

Psychology I
- Teach students answers to the fascinating question of why human beings behave as they do.
- Students explore the role of our biological makeup and our social environment in influencing how we respond as we do to a wide variety of daily situations.
- Students study famous experiments and psychological theories in an attempt to discover why people develop as they do behaviorally.

Psychology II
- Teach students that human behavior is a product of nature and nurture; that we act as we do because of our biological makeup and our social interactions.
- Introduce students to the most current interpretations of the nature of the human condition and how the greatest scholars in Psychology in past years have explained the workings of the human mind.

Sociology of the Family
- Teach students how to understand their position in the family.
- Students learn about Individual Development, Communication, Media Influences, Dating, Sexuality, and Adulthood.

HAILEY R. TRUMPP
113 Riverbend Road
Ft. Collins, CO 80521
(303) 224-1449

OBJECTIVE
Resource Teacher

EDUCATION
MS, Special Education, 1974
University of Northern Colorado, Greeley, CO

BS, Special Education, 1970
University of Northern Colorado, Greeley, CO

SPECIAL CREDENTIALS
Colorado Teaching Credential, Physical Education, Life

COMMUNITY SERVICE
Leader, Girl Scouts of America

PROFESSIONAL EXPERIENCE

RESOURCE TEACHER   1974-present
Ft. Collins High School, Ft. Collins, CO

- Teach reading and math to students requiring remedial work, using special help programs to improve scholastic level.

- Administer achievement tests and evaluate test results to discover level of language and math skills.

- Apply lesson techniques designed for short attention spans.

- Select and teach reading material and math problems related to everyday life of individual students.

- Confer with school counselors and staff to obtain additional testing information and gain insight on student behavior disorders affecting learning process.

- Design special help programs for low achievers and encourage parent-teacher cooperation.

- Attend professional meetings, write reports, and maintain records.

CARLI S. BUTLER
143 Ridgecrest Drive
Ft. Collins, CO 80525
(303) 223-1123

OBJECTIVE
Science Teacher

EDUCATION
BS, Biology, 1979
Colorado State University, Ft. Collins, CO

Teacher's Certification Program, 1974
University of Northern Colorado, Greeley, CO

CREDENTIALS
Colorado Secondary, **Science, 1974**
Colorado Secondary, **Elementary Education, 1974**

PROFESSIONAL EXPERIENCE
SCIENCE TEACHER   1974-present
Blevins Junior High School, Poudre R-1 School District, Ft. Collins, CO
- Teach Science courses to students, Grades 7-9.

Life Science, Physical Science, Bellwether Science
- Teach Life Science, which includes measurement, methods of science, survey of living organisms, and ecology in a laboratory setting.
- Teach Physical Science, which includes basic physical principles, basic chemical principles, and concepts related to energy.
- Teach Bellwether Science topics, which include aviation, scuba diving, rocketry, astronomy, insect collecting, and the study of birds.

Earth Science
- Teach students lessons concerning the planet we live on and our outer-space environment.
- Teach students in a laboratory-based environment the lithosphere, the hydrosphere, the atmosphere, the solar system, and the universe.
- Educate students on careers that are built around these disciplines.

Biology
- Teach students how to understand their living world using extensive laboratories to supplement lecture/reading activities.
- Teach lessons in cell biology, genetics and reproduction, study of five major kingdoms, and ecology.

JILLIAN ANNE HARTELL
1750 Sheeley Drive
Ft. Collins, CO 80524
(303) 224-6167

Objective: Social Studies Teacher

EDUCATION
BS, Social Studies, 1979
Colorado State University, Ft. Collins, CO

Teacher's Certification Program, 1974
University of Northern Colorado, Greeley, CO

CREDENTIALS
Colorado Secondary, **Social Studies, 1974**
Colorado Secondary, **Elementary Education, 1974**

PROFESSIONAL EXPERIENCE
SOCIAL STUDIES TEACHER   1974-present
Ft. Collins High School, Poudre R-1 School District, Ft. Collins, CO
- Teach courses in United States History, World History, and Anthropology to students, Grades 10-12.

United States History
- Teach students how to examine significant events and individuals in American History with emphasis on the period from 1870 to the present.
- Educate students in a chronological survey of the political, economic, and social development of the United States.

World History
- Teach students the development of Western civilization.
- Students learn about the ancient period, emphasizing the Greeks and Romans, through the European Renaissance of the 1500s.
- Teach students World History through the 1600s and continue to the present with emphasis on the major revolutions of the early modern and modern eras.

Anthropology
- Teach students awareness of and appreciation for the rich diversity of human behavior and beliefs.
- Examine the physical and cultural origins and development of the human species, taking us back in time some three million years.
- Students investigate techniques and evidence used to formulate theories about prehistoric and modern people who possess lifestyles different from our own.

VINCENT R. GILLIAN
210 Taft Hill Road
Ft. Collins, CO 80521
(303) 223-1167

Objective: Social Studies Teacher

EDUCATION
BS, Social Studies, 1979
Colorado State University, Ft. Collins, CO

Teacher's Certification Program, 1974
University of Northern Colorado, Greeley, CO

CREDENTIALS
Colorado Secondary, Social Studies, 1974
Colorado Secondary, Elementary Education, 1974

PROFESSIONAL EXPERIENCE
SOCIAL STUDIES TEACHER 1974-present
Blevins Junior High School, Poudre R-1 School District, Ft. Collins, CO
• Teach Social Studies to students, Grades 7-9.

World Geography/Cultures
• Teach students how to organize and to analyze information about world cultures from the Middle East, Asia, Europe, Africa, and South America.
• Emphasize physical geography skills and a knowledge of the cultural components of each area studied.

Early American History
• Teach students American history from the early fifteenth century until 1877.
• Content is organized around specific themes, and particular emphasis is given to the development, reinforcement, and application of specific skills.

Civics
• Prepare students to become informed and responsible citizens by increasing their knowledge and participatory skills needed to assume the responsibilities and enjoy the opportunities of adult citizenship.
• Emphasis is placed on the legal, economic, and political system in the United States.

PREVIOUS EMPLOYMENT HISTORY
Social Studies Teacher, Poudre R-1 School District, Ft. Collins, CO   1974-79

FRANCHESKA S. BREWSTER

665 Shields Avenue
Ft. Collins, CO 80521
(303) 223-1117

Objective: Social Studies Teacher

EDUCATION

BS, Social Studies, 1979
Colorado State University, Ft. Collins, CO

Teacher's Certification Program, 1974
University of Northern Colorado, Greeley, CO

CREDENTIALS

Colorado Secondary, Social Studies, 1974
Colorado Secondary, Elementary Education, 1974

PROFESSIONAL EXPERIENCE

SOCIAL STUDIES TEACHER   1974-present
Lincoln Junior High School, Poudre R-1 School District, Ft. Collins, CO
• Teach Social Studies to students, Grades 7-9.

Ft. Collins History
• Teach students the history of their hometown including many of the early men and women who helped create the city.
• Study and explore buildings and sites as well as the story of the fort and the Old town areas using slides, maps, and group discussion.

Colorado History and Geography
• Teach students about Colorado and its unique past including the early Native Americans, explorers, fur trappers, miners, ranchers, and settlers.
• Study modern Colorado and present and future concerns of both the state and the city of Ft. Collins.
• Teach students the physical regions of Colorado using slides, maps, and discussions.
• Discuss and explore in depth landforms, climate, sources of water, and general geography of the state of Colorado, as well as plant and animal life.

PREVIOUS EMPLOYMENT HISTORY

Social Studies Teacher, Poudre R-1 School District, Ft. Collins, CO   1974-79

GEORGE PAUL STEINER
1250 Lemay Drive
Ft. Collins, CO 80524
(303) 224-0098

Objective: Social Studies Teacher

EDUCATION
BS, Social Studies, 1979
Colorado State University, Ft. Collins, CO

Teacher's Certification Program, 1974
University of Northern Colorado, Greeley, CO

CREDENTIALS
Colorado Secondary, **Social Studies, 1974**
Colorado Secondary, **Elementary Education, 1974**

PROFESSIONAL EXPERIENCE
SOCIAL STUDIES TEACHER   1974-present
Rocky Mountain High School, Poudre R-1 School District, Ft. Collins, CO
- Teach courses in World Cultures and Geography, Political Science and Russian History to students, Grades 10-12.

World Cultures and Geography
- Teach students geography, culture, economy, and politics in major world regions.
- Students study regional issues that affect people in the world using historic experiences and the cultural perspectives of each region.
- Studies include relationships of each world region to others including the USA.

Political Science
- Teach students the Political System of the United States and the role of the individual within it.
- Students learn rights and responsibilities of citizenship through a "hands-on" approach.
- Emphasize how the individual can use the power of citizen action at the local, state, and national level.
- Investigate practical and theoretical issues of the American political system.

Russian History
- Students examine the history of Russia until the present, including Russian culture and literature.
- Students develop a historical perspective on Russian policies and be able to compare Russian and American cultures.

JENNA SUZANNA FRANK
3210 Chaparral Street
Fillmore, CA 93015
(805) 524-7123

OBJECTIVE
Special Education Teacher

EDUCATION
Multiple Subject Teaching Credential, 1987
California Lutheran University, GPA: 4.0

MA, Special Education, 1986
California State University, Northridge, CA

BA, Special Education, 1975
California State University, Fullerton, CA

PROFESSIONAL EXPERIENCE
SPECIAL EDUCATION TEACHER   1987-present
Rio Mesa School, Ventura, CA
- Teach severe physically handicapped children community access, domestic/self care skills, recreation/leisure activities, vocational training, and academic skills.

RESOURCE SPECIALIST TEACHER (Grades 9-12)   1986-87
Santa Paula High School, Santa Paula, CA
- Taught learning handicapped students Global Concepts, United States History, United States Government, Driver's Education, Health Education, Career Education, Science, and Mathematics.
- Administered standardized tests to students to measure academic growth and for their Individualized Educational Programs (IEPs).
- Participate in the IEP conferences with parents and professionals.
- Implemented behavior management strategies for students needing motivation in positive behavior.

AFFILIATIONS
Member, Special Education Association

LOCATION OF PLACEMENT PAPERS
Educational Careers
Counseling and Career Services
California State University at Northridge
Northridge, CA 91330
(818) 885-2932

PAULINA S. SLOSSON
259 Shields Street
Ft. Collins, CO 80524
(303) 225-4457

OBJECTIVE
Special Education Teacher

EDUCATION
MA, Special Education, 1970
University of Northern Colorado, Greeley, CO

BA, English, Pennsylvania State University,
University Park, PA, 1967

SPECIAL TEACHING CREDENTIALS
- Learning Handicapped Specialist Teaching Credential, Life
- Single Subject Teaching Credential, English, Life
- Secondary School Special Education Credential, Life

PROFESSIONAL EXPERIENCE
IRISH ELEMENTARY SCHOOL, Ft. Collins, CO   1987-present
Special Education Classroom Teacher
- Set clear specific student-centered objectives at appropriate level of difficulty.
- Prepare plans that incorporate district curriculum objectives and approved texts.
- Demonstrate systematic long-term planning.
- Use instructional techniques appropriate to students and content of lessons.
- Select visual, auditory, and kinesthetic activities.
- Assess learning needs and abilities of each student.
- Design objectives and lessons based on knowledge of students.
- Develop Individualized Educational Program (IEP) based on knowledge derived from assessment as required by the state of colorado.
- Allocate appropriate amount of time for instruction and organize materials to maximize learning opportunities.
- Arrange physical environment to make learning appropriate for students.
- Teach skills for critical thinking, problem solving, decision making, and independent learning by students.
- Design and use evaluation strategies congruent with teaching techniques, learning objectives, content, and students.
- Communicate student's progress effectively to student and parent/guardian.
- Communicate expectations for student learning and provide opportunities for student's successes.

- More -

PROFESSIONAL PROFILE

- Encourage student expressions of respect for one another and self.
- Convey enjoyment and enthusiasm for teaching and serve as a positive role model in the school environment.
- Treat individuals with respect and dignity.
- Establish a nurturing and caring environment.
- Establish conditions under which students exercise self-discipline, honesty, leadership, and citizenship.
- Participate in staff development activities, continuing education courses, and professional organizations to keep abreast of current teaching methods.
- Demonstrate a concern for student health and safety.

PROFESSIONAL AFFILIATIONS

- Association for Children and Adults with Learning Disabilities (ACALD) - Colorado, Denver Chapter
- Council on Exceptional Children - Mental Retardation Division, Early Childhood Division
- National Down Syndrome Congress

EMPLOYMENT HISTORY

Substitute Teacher, Poudre R-1 School District, Ft. Collins, CO   1970-74
Group Home Coordinator, Children's Home, Seattle, WA   Summers 1965-70

MELANNIE P. PULLMAN
909 South Avenue
Memphis, TN 38126
(901) 774-4556

OBJECTIVE
Special Education Teacher

PROFESSIONAL EXPERIENCE

RUTLEDGE CITY COLLEGE, Memphis, TN   1987-present
Essential Skills Instructor
- Assess students' individualized reading and writing skills and needs.
- Direct instruction in reading and writing skills.
- Supervise students in reading lab.
- Direct and supervise instructional aide's work in class and office.
- Evaluate student progress.

RHODES SCHOOL, Memphis, TN   1982-87
Coordinator of Education (1985-87)
- Supervised and evaluated teachers and instructional aides.
- Coordinated student intake, assessment, and class placement.
- Monitored and evaluated instructional program and curriculum guidelines.
- Developed and facilitated staff in-service.
- Reported to Board of Directors on education program implementation and new program development.
- Interfaced and consulted with public agencies.
- Facilitated transition from one administrator to another.

Special Education Day Class Teacher (1982-85)
- Directed instruction in academic and independent living skills for young adults with developmental disability, ages 16-22 years.
- Developed and implemented individualized educational plans.
- Monitored student progress and maintained student records.
- Coordinated community vocational experiences with agencies and school sites.

MEMPHIS RESIDENTIAL PROGRAM, Memphis, TN   1976-84
Educational Consultant (1983-84)
- Developed and implemented in-service training program for independent living skills instructors.
- Evaluated independent living skills instructors' performance and classes.
- Provided ongoing consultation, resources and materials to instructors.

- More -

PROFESSIONAL EXPERIENCE (Continued)

Sensory Motor Program Supervisor (1981-82)
- Supervised staff therapists.
- Assessed and evaluated clients' needs.
- Designed and implemented behavioral goals and objectives for clients.
- Planned and conducted in-service training for staff and school faculty.
- Evaluated and revised program goals.
- Provided direct service to clients with developmental disability, ages 7-18.

EDUCATION

MA, Special Education, in progress
University of California, Santa Barbara, CA

BA, English, Pennsylvania State University,
University Park, PA, 1967

SPECIAL TRAINING

- Learning Handicapped Specialist Teaching Credential, Life
- Single Subject Teaching Credential, English, Life
- Community College Basic Skills Credential, Life

PROFESSIONAL AFFILIATIONS

- Association for Children and Adults with Learning Disabilities
  (ACLD) - California, Santa Barbara Chapter
- Council on Exceptional Children - Mental Retardation
  Division, Early Childhood Division
- National Down Syndrome Congress

EMPLOYMENT HISTORY

Substitute Teacher, Maricopa County Schools, Austin, TX   1973-75
Res. Group Home Coordinator, Children's Industrial Home, Bellingham, WA   1972
Special Education Resource Teacher
Camp Springs Elementary School Bellingham, WA   1970-71
Special Education Day Class Teacher, Severely Emotionally Disabled
Edgemeade School, Seattle, WA   1969-70

STEVEN R. ORTEGA
3412 North Overland Trail
Ft. Collins, CO 80521
(303) 224-0045

OBJECTIVE
Technology Teacher

EDUCATION
BS, Physics, 1979
Colorado State University, Ft. Collins, CO

Teacher's Certification Program, 1974
University of Northern Colorado, Greeley, CO

CREDENTIALS
Colorado Secondary, Technology/Physics, 1978
Colorado Secondary, Elementary Education, 1979

PROFESSIONAL EXPERIENCE

TECHNOLOGY TEACHER   1978-present
Rocky Mountain High School, Poudre R-1 School District, Ft. Collins, CO
- Teach courses in Physics and Aerospace Science to students, Grades 10-12.
- Combined cooperative learning, problem solving, learning contracts, guest speakers, evaluation techniques, and student reports that increased comprehension, study skills, classroom participation and motivation.

Applied Physics and Technology I
- Teach students scientific principles in applied physics with video and hands-on laboratory experiences with mechanical, fluid, thermal, and electrical systems.
- Students learn a broad knowledge base of principles that underlie modern technical systems, giving them career flexibility.
- Students visit industries as part of this course.

Applied Physics and Technology II
- Teach students Physics related to Momentum, Waves and Vibrations, Energy Converters, Transducers, Radiation, Optical Systems, and Time Constants.
- Students visit industries and learn instrumentation, related theory, applied math.

Aerospace Science/Technology
- Teach students the history of aviation, aerodynamics, weather, propulsion systems, flight control, guidance, map reading and navigation, missiles, rockets, and satellites.

RANDOLPH S. MARSHALL
2595 South Taft Hill Road
Ft. Collins, CO 80521
(303) 224-4432

OBJECTIVE
Technology Teacher

EDUCATION
BS, Architecture, 1979
Colorado State University, Ft. Collins, CO

Teacher's Certification Program, 1974
University of Northern Colorado, Greeley, CO

CREDENTIALS
Colorado Secondary, **Technology/Architecture, 1978**
Colorado Secondary, **Elementary Education, 1979**

PROFESSIONAL EXPERIENCE

TECHNOLOGY TEACHER   1978-present
Ft. Collins High School, Poudre R-1 School District, Ft. Collins, CO
- Teach courses in Architecture and Communication Systems to students Grades 10-12 who are interested in a career in Engineering.
- Combined cooperative learning, problem solving, learning contracts, guest speakers, evaluation techniques, and student reports that increased comprehension, study skills, classroom participation and motivation.

Architecture
- Students explore residential and commercial architecture.
- Teach students about structures design, building, and testing.
- Instruct students on how to manufacture scale models of houses, buildings, and bridges, using tools, machines, and materials.

Communication Systems
- Teach students and understanding of current and future trends of technology and graphic communications.
- Students explore drafting, graphic design, desktop publishing, and CAD through interpretation of mechanically drawn designs.
- Students learn to visualize and think precisely and creatively to improve their technical imagination.

HARRISON R. RANEY
256 Lake Street
Ft. Collins, CO 80524
(303) 224-2210

Objective: Theatre Arts Teacher

EDUCATION
BA, Theatre Arts, 1979
Colorado State University, Ft. Collins, CO

Teacher's Certification Program, 1974
University of Northern Colorado, Greeley, CO

CREDENTIALS
Colorado Secondary, **Theatre Arts, 1974**
Colorado Secondary, **Elementary Education, 1974**

PROFESSIONAL EXPERIENCE

THEATRE ARTS TEACHER   1974-present
Ft. Collins High School, Poudre R-1 School District, Ft. Collins, CO
- Teach Musical Theatre Production and Creative Writing: Short Stories and Drama to students, Grades 10-12.

Musical Theater Production—Visual Arts
- Art students learn to design and create the sets, lighting design, publicity materials, and program.
- Students are taught the importance of teamwork and attend rehearsals and construction meetings while producing the fall musical.

Musical Theater Production—Language Arts
- Teach all aspects of performing and producing a major musical production to talented singer, actor, dancer, orchestral player, and artist students.
- Students study the play learning thematic concepts, character development, and performance and production skills.
- All students participate in the final production.

Creative Writing: Short Stories and Drama
- Teach gifted students how to write original short stories, a one-act play, and a personal narrative.
- Students demonstrate the ability to listen attentively to others' readings, to respond honestly in criticizing others' writings, and to accept criticism.

ISABELLA KANE
231 Boardwalk Way
Ft. Collins, CO 80526
(303) 224-1109

OBJECTIVE
Visually Impaired Teacher position

EDUCATION
MA, Special Education, 1974
University of Northern Colorado, Greeley, CO

BA, Special Education, 1970
University of Northern Colorado, Greeley, CO

SPECIAL CREDENTIALS
Learning Handicapped Specialist Teaching Credential, Life
Multiple Subject Teaching Credential, K-12, Life

PROFESSIONAL EXPERIENCE
TEACHER, VISUALLY IMPAIRED   1974-present
Poudre R-1 School District, Ft. Collins, CO
- Teach elementary and secondary school subjects and daily living skills to visually impaired students.
- Instruct students in reading and writing, using magnification equipment and large print material or braille system.
- Confer with parents, administrator, testing specialists, social worker, and others to develop Individualized Educational Program for students.
- Plan curriculum and prepare lessons and instructional materials, according to grade level of students.
- Transcribe lessons and other materials into braille for blind students and large print for low vision students.
- Review completed assignments, using braille writer, slate and stylus, or computer.
- Arrange for and conduct field trips designed to promote experiential learning.
- Instruct students in academic subject areas and daily living skills, such as hygiene, safety, and food preparation.
- Encourage students to participate in verbal and sensory classroom learning experiences to ensure their comprehension of subject matter, development of social skills, and ability to identify objects encountered in daily living.
- Meet with parents to discuss how parents can encourage student's independence and well-being and to provide guidance in using community resources.
- Counsel students and teach braille to individuals with sight.

GARY RILEY SAMSON
221 Whedbee Street
Ft. Collins, CO 80524
(303) 224-2877

OBJECTIVE
Teacher, Vocational Training

EDUCATION
MA, Special Education, 1974
University of Northern Colorado, Greeley, CO

BA, Special Education, 1970
University of California, Santa Barbara, CA

SPECIAL CREDENTIALS
Learning Handicapped Specialist Teaching Credential, Life
Multiple Subject Teaching Credential, K-12, Life
Certified by the county, state, and federal government

PROFESSIONAL EXPERIENCE
TEACHER, VOCATIONAL TRAINING   1974-present
Poudre R-1 School District, Ft. Collins, CO
- Teach vocational skills to handicapped students.
- Confer with students, parents, therapists, school personnel, and others to plan vocational training that meets needs, interests, and abilities of students.
- Instructs students in personal-social skills and work-related behaviors.
- Develop work opportunities that allow students to experience success in performing tasks of increasing difficulty and teach work values; self-improvement, independence, dependability, productivity, and pride of workmanship.
- Conduct field trips to enable students to learn about job activities and explore work environments.
- Teach students food preparation, gardening, woodworking, and building maintenance.

PROFESSIONAL AFFILIATIONS
Council on Exceptional Children - Mental Retardation Division

PREVIOUS EMPLOYMENT HISTORY
Teacher, Vocational Training, Goleta Valley School District, Goleta, CA   1970-74

CHARLOTTE I. RANDALL
3210 LaPorte Avenue
Ft. Collins, CO 80521
(303) 224-2138

OBJECTIVE
Urban Horticulture Instructor

EDUCATION
Colorado Vocational Teaching credential, 1979

MA, Urban Horticulture, 1979
Colorado State University, Ft. Collins, CO

BA, Urban Horticulture, 1975
University of Colorado, Boulder, CO

PROFESSIONAL EXPERIENCE

URBAN HORTICULTURE INSTRUCTOR   1979-present
Front Range Community College, Ft. Collins, CO
- Teach college level courses in Urban Horticulture on a daily basis.
- Maintain and operate program greenhouse and labs.
- Develop course curriculum and advise faculty and staff in the Urban Horticulture Department.
- Select textbooks for courses offered.
- Serve on committees and provide continued leadership to part-time faculty.

AFFILIATION
Member, Urban Horticulture Society, 1979

PREVIOUS EMPLOYMENT HISTORY
Urban Horticulture Instructor, Aims Community College, Greeley, CO   1975-79
Teacher's Aide, University of Colorado, Boulder, CO   1972-75

WILLIAM B. MADISON
2178 McConnel Way
Ft. Collins, CO 80521
(303) 224-1124

OBJECTIVE
Vice President

EDUCATION
PhD, Education Administration, 1983
University of Northern Colorado, Greeley, CO

MA, Education Administration, 1979
University of Northern Colorado, Greeley, CO

BA, English, 1974
University of Denver, Denver, CO

PROFESSIONAL EXPERIENCE

VICE PRESIDENT, Larimer County Center   1983-present
Front Range Community College, Ft. Collins, CO
- Plan, direct, supervise, and evaluate all campus and related outreach functions.
- Serve as the spokesperson for the College in the local community.
- Direct strategic planning process for the campus including educational program, facilities, and budget development.
- Determine and communicate administrative operational goals.
- Provide for evaluation of employees and programs.
- Ensure observance of college policies and procedures.
- Recommend campus personnel for employment.
- Implement college affirmative action plan.
- Provide for staff development and expansion, utilization, and upkeep of facilities.

COMMUNITY SERVICE
Board Member, Rotary Club of Larimer County
Social Chair, Hospice of Ft. Collins
President, Front Range Community College School Goal Committee

PREVIOUS EMPLOYMENT HISTORY
Dean of Student Services, Aims Community College, Greeley, CO   1979-83
English Instructor, Front Range Community College, Boulder, CO   1974-79

GEORGE CHARLES WYATT
3209 LaPorte Avenue
Ft. Collins, CO 80524
(303) 224-2194

OBJECTIVE
Water/Wastewater Technology Instructor

EDUCATION
Licensure, Water and Wastewater Treatment, 1974

MS, Wastewater Management, 1979
University of Northern Colorado, Greeley, CO

BS, Wastewater Management, 1974
University of Denver, Denver, CO

PROFESSIONAL EXPERIENCE

WATER/WASTEWATER TECHNOLOGY INSTRUCTOR   1979-present
Front Range Community College, Ft. Collins, CO
- Teach college courses including Unit Processes of Water Treatment, Unit Processes of Wastewater Treatment, Hydraulics, Pumps and Motors, Chemistry and Associate Water/Wastewater labs.

- Work closely with the water/wastewater sectors of the community to arrange and supervise internship portions of the program.

- Advise staff members and serve on committees concerning wastewater issues.

- Recruit wastewater students.

COMMUNITY SERVICE
Volunteer, Colorado Health Department

PREVIOUS EMPLOYMENT HISTORY
Wastewater Technology Instructor, Aims College, Greeley, CO   1978-79
Wastewater Technologist, City of Denver, Denver, CO   1974-77

Index to Resume
Samples by Job Title